MW00807236

CFS
Contemporary Freudian Society

IPTAR

ICP+P

IPBOOKS.net
International Psychoanalytic Books

NEW DIRECTIONS

PsiAN
Psychotherapy Action Network

# Contributors

**Libby Bachhuber, LCSW,** provides psychoanalytic psychotherapy and supervision through her independent practice in Chicago and serves as clinical associate faculty at the Chicago Center for Psychoanalysis. Her work engages with the social, political, and spiritual concerns that run through patients' lives, including issues involving gender, race, and climate. She has facilitated reflective processes with a range of groups, including activists, elementary school teachers, and psychotherapists.

**Catherine Baker-Pitts, PhD, LCSW,** is a psychotherapist in private practice in New York City who cares a lot about body liberation, gender expansiveness, sexual freedom, and body nonconformity. She offers gender-affirmative care and practices from a harm-reduction model. She earned degrees from Duke University, the University of Texas at Austin, and New York University, in addition to multiple postgraduate psychoanalytic certificates. She has published scholarly articles and chapters for books in the field of gender and sexuality. She is a graduate and guest faculty at New Directions, a writing program with a psychoanalytic edge in Washington, DC.

**Philip Brunetti** writes innovative fiction and poetry, and much of his work has been published in various online or paper literary magazines, including the *Boiler*, the *Wax Paper*, and *Identity Theory*. His debut novel, *Newer Testaments*, published in 2020 by Atmosphere Press, has been described in the Independent Book Review as "an innovative existential novel told through hallucinatory poetics" and is available for purchase.

**Richard Grose, PhD,** is a psychoanalyst who is a member of *ROOM*'s editorial board and book review editor for *ROOM*. He is interested in how culture and psychoanalysis can illuminate each other. He has a private practice in psychotherapy and psychoanalysis in Manhattan.

**Mirjam Meerschwam Hadar** translates Hebrew texts on philosophy, psychoanalysis, and culture studies, and sometimes fiction, into English. She works in Tel Aviv and sometimes in Amsterdam.

**Matt A. Hanson** is a writer, journalist, and editor based in Istanbul. His fiction has appeared in the *Write Launch*, *Underwood Press*, the *Bosphorus Review of Books*, and *Panorama: The Journal of Travel, Place, and Nature* and is forthcoming for *The Skewies: An Award Anthology* and the Summer 2023 issue of *Washington Square Review*. He is the founder of the indie digital publishing platform FictiveMag.com.

**Naftally Israeli** is a clinical psychologist from Jerusalem and a candidate in the Israeli Psychoanalytic Society. He earned his PhD from Bar-Ilan University after studying in the Psychoanalysis and Hermeneutics program there. His book, *Emotional Language* (2019, in Hebrew), summarizes his research about the interconnections between language and experience. He also works with children in his clinic. He answers their questions and writes about psychological issues in *Einayim*, a monthly magazine for children of ages six to thirteen. He is mainly concerned about their future in the catastrophic political situation in Israel nowadays.

**Anaís Martinez Jimenez** is a PhD candidate in comparative literature working on poetics, psychoanalytic theory, and race and gender studies at Princeton University. She is an analyst in training at the National Psychological Association for Psychoanalysis in New York City. She was born and raised in the international border area between Tijuana, Baja California, and San Diego, California, and while growing up in Mexico she crossed the border daily for sixteen years to go to school in the United States.

**Murad Khan, MD,** works with Yale students using pharmacotherapy, individual therapy, and group therapy modalities. They use their personal and professional experiences in teaching, research, and community organizing to acknowledge their implication in oppressive institutions. A current APA Division 39 Scholar and APsA Teacher's Academy Fellow, they have presented on the mental health concerns of QTBIPOC for the American Psychiatric Association, the American Psychological Association, the American Psychoanalytic Association, and the Association of LGBTQ+ Psychiatrists. They are first author of the chapter on Gender and Sexual Identities in *The Psychiatry Resident Handbook—How to Thrive in Training.*

**Destiney Kirby** is a senior medical student in the Bronx who is pursuing a career in family medicine and public health. She is an emerging creative nonfiction essayist who explores the parallels between her past life and the one she created in her young adult years. Her work has been published in *Pulse-Voices from the Heart of Medicine* and *Ad Libitum Art & Literary Magazine*.

**Linda Michaels, PsyD, MBA,** is the chair and cofounder of the Psychotherapy Action Network (PsiAN), a nonprofit that advocates for therapies that create lasting change. She is also a consulting editor of *Psychoanalytic Inquiry*, clinical associate faculty at the Chicago Center for Psychoanalysis, and a fellow of the Lauder Institute Global MBA program. She has a private practice in Chicago, working with adults and couples.

**Mia Muratori** was born in Heidelberg, Germany. She studied painting at the Art Students League in New York with Robert Beauchamp, ceramics at the Ceramics Institute in Faenza, Italy, and received her MFA from the University of Delaware. Muratori exhibits nationally and internationally. Her work reflects thoughts on the evolution of consciousness, the construction, destruction, and reconstruction of popular myths and symbols, and the understanding of universal themes.

**Stephanie Niu** is a poet and digital storyteller from Marietta, Georgia. She is the author of *Survived By*, winner of the 2023 Host Publications Chapbook Prize, and *She Has Dreamt Again of Water*, winner of the 2021 Diode Chapbook Contest. Her poems have appeared in *Copper Nickel*, *Waxwing*, *Ecotone*, the *Georgia Review*, and elsewhere. She is currently completing a Fulbright scholarship on immigration and labor history on Christmas Island in the Indian Ocean.

**Diane Raptosh's** collection *American Amnesiac* (Etruscan Press), was longlisted for the 2013 National Book Award in poetry. The recipient of three fellowships in literature from the Idaho Commission on the Arts, she served as the Boise Poet Laureate (2013) as well as the Idaho Writer-in-Residence (2013–2016). In 2018 she won the Idaho Governor's Award for Excellence in the Arts. She teaches literature and creative writing and codirects the program in Criminal Justice/Prison Studies at the College of Idaho. Her newest chapbook, *Hand Signs from Eternity's Yurt*, was published in June 2022 (Kelsay Books). dianeraptosh.com

**Chaim Rochester** is a clinical psychology PhD student at Pacifica Graduate Institute, as well as a writer, musician, and executive recovery coach. Inspired by the work of Lacan, Fanon, and Andre Green, Chaim's clinical and research interests center on themes of alienation and liminality and the ways in which psychoanalysis might be used to address the impossibility of cohesion under late capitalism.

**Shegofa Shahbaz** is a university student. She was the director of an organization in Afghanistan with programs for women's and girls' empowerment, but when the Taliban took over Afghanistan, that program could not continue, and she fled Afghanistan. Besides her own organization activities, Shahbaz works as a volunteer with many other organizations. She has very big dreams and is developing her abilities and skills for the day she goes back to Afghanistan to work for women's and girls' empowerment. She believes that one day Afghanistan will be free and peaceful and a developed country.

**Reuben Sinha** is an artist and an art teacher in New York City. His awards include the MacDowell Traveling Scholarship and a Fulbright Fellowship. He used both grants to return to India to study and paint. These trips awakened and challenged his notions that art can only exist in a cultural context, i.e., his art is always trying to bridge his two cultures. He was the founder and executive director of artHARLEM, a not-for-profit community arts organization that produced the Harlem Open Artist Studio Tour. He has taught drawing and anatomy at the Art Students League of New York and Spring Studio. His work is in numerous private and public collections in India, Russia, Germany, Lebanon, Japan, and the United States, including Columbia University and the Fulbright House, New Delhi.

# Contents

**Hattie Myers**
hattie@analytic-room.com



# Gateways

**"Disorientation becomes a gateway to something else."**

—Foluke Taylor, 2023

"It has been almost two years since we were waiting for you to take action. We expected you to not be just a viewer," Shegofa Shahbaz wrote to the UN. But because she wasn't sure the UN would read a letter written by a twenty-year-old college student sent on behalf of all the Afghan girls whose lives have been shattered, Shahbaz sent it to *ROOM*, hoping we might publish it, hoping it might find its way to the UN. Of course we will publish it, we told her. We will publish it in English and Dari so that other Afghan girls might find strength and hope through these words that they might be heard—that they will be recognized.

In their "portrait of an analyst as a young man," Murad Khan shows us how, from an early age, they also had to learn how to recognize and thread a needle through precarious forces. "We are all caught in a three-dimensional matrix, under forces that push us in different directions depending on the context we're in at any given moment," writes Khan in **"Re/calibrating"** their quilted memoir of surviving family, country, medical school, and professional community. From Jerusalem, Naftally Israeli describes the seemingly insurmountable forces that have pushed his homeland into "apparent madness." From the prophet Isaiah to the analyst Donald Meltzer, Israeli's essay, **"From Exclusion to Erasure,"** delves into the heart of darkness, a crazy quilt that has become Israel. "A complex and integrated view of the truth cannot be maintained by excluding entire swaths of the population from ethical (not just ideological) recognition," he writes. "For recognition to be truly ethical [...] it should be translated into action." For Israeli, ethical action in his country must translate into new legal definitions relevant to unrecognized minority groups, new forms of political representation, and redistribution of resources.

From Afghanistan to Pakistan, from Israel to the United States, the authors in *ROOM 6.23* show us how weaponizing legal systems can take many forms. **"When Talkspace Sued PsiAN and Me"** lets us in on the fury and terror Linda Michaels experienced when Talkspace attempted to use the courts as an instrument to silence her. In **"Rape on Trial,"** Catherine Baker-Pitts recalls when she was called upon to be a witness in a rape trial for a client of hers and saw what we all were given to see last month, that "the strategies of legal defense rely on retrograde rape myths." Like Shegofa's letter to the UN, these essays, which were written from the frontlines, are pleas for recognition. And beyond the demand for recognition, they are pleas for the kind of ethical action that will lead to structural change.

In their essays, Matt Hanson and Destiney Kirby also describe the material and psychic experience of being excluded and included. As a journalist, Hanson's livelihood depended upon his accepting work for government-censored publications. In **"Adventures in Turkish Journalism,"** he writes how he was "[m]uted by a lingering, doomsday climate of political fear, civic space [...] overshadowed by the blockage of free assembly and the silencing of free speech." Having freed himself from this stranglehold, Hanson is now "working harder than ever toward an end that [he has] never cared less to define."

Destiney Kirby's **"On Hair Care"** becomes a metaphor for describing how confusing and what hard work "caring" can be in the course of defining identity. Kirby recalls, beginning at age eight, being dropped off by her white mother at Black hair salons, where she wanted nothing more than for "the chemicals to strip away every ounce of Blackness they could find so I could finally be considered *beautiful*." At the same time, she remembers desperately wanting to please the stylists (her first "Black aunties"), who insisted (every time) that she keep "a little texture in." Looking back, Kirby can see "two truths [...] the part of [herself] that was deeply aching for love and acceptance [...] [and] [...] a future of new beginnings, discomfort, and growth: a future filled with acceptance and discovery."

Along with these authors who are tackling recalibration and relocation in physical and psychic spaces, this issue of *ROOM* also showcases those who find themselves with a lack of community. Chaim Rochester's **"Carol"** is an elegy to a single woman and to all those swept to the margins "who did not survive their war against the crushing indifference of the modern world." Rochester, who himself has "traversed the spaces between the purgatory of fearful isolation, the conflict of polluted empathy, and the acceptance of powerless solidarity," speaks of the "silent recognition" one person lends to another's survival. He cannot make sense of the fact that he is still here.

Like Rochester, Libby Bachhuber is trying to make sense of where she (and the field more generally) has landed post-pandemic. "Many of us are living with the echoes of unmourned losses and a flight to technology that began three years ago," she writes in **"What We Left Behind."** "We are left with forms of insularity and of distance communication that are partly chosen and partly habits we developed to cope." Bachhuber wonders what might come of remembering, of opening our feelings to what we have lost. She wonders whether a form of dissociation is at work, protecting us from the threat we felt that forced our adaptations. Her essay is more reverie than elegy, but like all the authors in *ROOM 6.23*, Bachhuber writes of trying to find her bearings.

"If disorientation is a gateway to something else," as Foluke Taylor writes in her book *Unruly Therapeutic: Black Feminist Writing and Practices in Living Room*, we must find a way "to let go of the idea that we already know—or should already know where we are going." "Recognizing our task," she tells us, "as *description* more than *knowing* creates therapeutic room."

*ROOM* was founded by a handful of disoriented analysts, artists, and writers who were spurred to speech after the 2016 US election. On behalf of the editorial board, the hundreds of writers, artists, poets, and activists who have filled *ROOM* over the last six years, and the thousands of readers in now more than 160 countries who have come through *ROOM*'s doors to join our community action, I want to break the "fourth wall" that usually frames these editorials and acknowledge the extraordinary analytic journey we have taken together as a growing community. I would like to make special note of how thrilled we all are that the International Psychoanalytic Association (the IPA) has awarded *ROOM* a first-place prize in honor of its "contribution to culture." I also want to take the opportunity to introduce Brent Matheny, who will be assuming the new role of managing editor; Elizabeth Kandall, who is joining Eugene Mahon as poetry editor; and Francesca Schwartz, *ROOM*'s art editor. I'd also like to give special thanks to Boyd Delancey, who is *ROOM*'s creative director and much more.

*ROOM* is a collective analytic practice. To borrow a phrase from the Black feminist psychotherapist Gail Lewis, it is "an ensemble of artifacts." Each magazine is a reflection of where we are now. Over time, the many *ROOM*s we have created together have become an analytic archive, a record of where we were and how we are moving into unknown and uncertain territory. Join us! We are open for submissions through September 1, 2023. ■

**Letters to *ROOM*:** Jenny Shepherd

**Shegofa Shahbaz**
shegofashahbaz81@gmail.com



# LETTER TO THE UNITED NATIONS

To the United Nations,

I am writing this letter on behalf of all Afghan girls.

I am Shegofa Shahbaz. I am twenty years old. I grew up among the dust and smoke of explosions, gunshots, fire, war, and sad stories. I grew up with fear. Fear of an explosion inside our classroom, fear of not seeing my family again, fear of losing my friends, and fear of losing my dreams. Beside all those sad stories in my life, I had a hope for a better future, but when the Taliban took the control of Afghanistan, my dreams were destroyed. Not only my dreams but the dream of all Afghan girls destroyed, and the page of history returned to twenty years ago. Now I have no hope for a better future in Afghanistan.

It has been almost two years that we have been waiting for you to take action. We expected you to not be just a viewer. In the past twenty years we have made progress in every area. We hoped that we would not go back, and we didn't even see this day in our dreams. The government falling at the hands of Taliban was the start of dark days in Afghanistan. Darkness in a country which was a member of the United Nations can be darkness in the world.

These days we hear that the United Nations is trying to recognize Taliban, want to accept them as a legal government. But here in Afghanistan, it is almost two years that we are not allowed to go to school and university, we have not had the right to work outside, we do not have the right to go to parks, and we have not even had the right to live as humans. We know that you know, that you are aware of this situation in Afghanistan, but we want you to not be silent. It is time to take action against this cruelty and injustice. We want you to not recognize Taliban. If you recognize them, you commit the greatest injustice against the people of Afghanistan.

In this modern era, in the time that all countries in the world are progressing, it is not fair that Afghanistan stay dark. Most of the countries in the world have achieved scientific progress. Humans are trying to find a place to live on other planets, but in Afghanistan, women and girls do not have basic human rights.

In past years, we witnessed all the crimes of Taliban. This group which has the authority in Afghanistan has committed inhuman crimes against the people of Afghanistan. They exploded the hospitals and educational centers, beheaded innocent people. If you recognize them, you will give legitimacy and rights to a criminal group. If you recognize them, you will do the greatest injustice against women and girls in Afghanistan.

5 May 2023
Shegofa Shahbaz

به سازمان ملل،

من این نامه را به نمایندگی از تمام دختران افغان مینویسم.

شگوفه شهباز هستم و بیست سال دارم . من در میان دود و خاک انفجار، گلوله های تفنگ ، آتش و جنگ بزرگ شده ام. من با یک دنیا ترس بزرگ شده ام. ترس ندیدن خانواده ام برای آخرین بار ، ترس انفجار داخل صنف درسی ، ترس از دست دادن دوستانم و ترس از دست دادن رویاهایم . در کنار همه ی داستانهای غمگین زندگی ام من امیدی برای فردای بهتر داشتم. اما وقتی افغانستان به دست طالبان سقوط کرد تمام رویاهایم نابود شد ، نه تنها رویاهای من بلکه رویاهای تمام دختران افغان نابود شد و صفحه ی تاریخ به بیست سال قبل ورق خورد.حالا هیچ امیدی برای فردای بهتر در افغانستان ندارم.

تقریبا دو سال است که منتظریم شما کاری کنید. ما از شما توقع داشتیم که فقط یک تماشاگر نباشید. ما در بیست سال گذشته در هر عرصه پیشرفت داشتیم ، امید داشتیم که دیگر به گذشته بر نخواهیم گشت . و حتی این روز را در رویاهای ما نمی دیدیم.سقوط حکومت در دست طالبان شروع روزهای تاریک در افغانستان بود. و تاریکی در کشوری که در گذشته عضو سازمان ملل بود میتواند تاریکی در جهان باشد.

این روزها میشنویم که سازمان ملل میخواهد طالبان را به رسمیت بشناسد. میخواهد گروه طالبان را به عنوان یک حکومت قانونی قبول کند. اما اینجا در افغانستان تقریبا دو سال می شود که ما اجازه رفتن به مکتب و دانشگاه را نداریم ، اجازه کار کردن در بیرون از خانه را نداریم ، اجازه رفتن به جاهای تفریحی را نداریم و حتی اجازه ی زندگی به عنوان یک انسان را نداریم . ما میدانیم که شما میدانید، شما از این اوضاع افغانستان آگاه هستید. اما ما از شما می خواهیم که خاموش نباشید، حالا وقت این است که در مقابل این بی عدالتی و ظلم کاری کنید. ما از شما میخواهیم که طالبان را به رسمیت نشناسید. اگر طالبان را به رسمیت بشناسید بزرگترین ظلم را در حق مردم افغانستان میکنید.

در این عصر مدرن، در زمانی که همه ی کشورهای جهان در حال پیشرفت اند این عادلانه نیست که افغانستان تاریک بماند. بیشتر کشورهای جهان پیشرفت علمی کرده اند و انسانها به جستجوی مکانی برای زندگی در سیاره های دیگر هستند. اما اینجا در افغانستان زنان و دختران ابتدایی ترین حق زندگی شان را ندارند.

در سالهای قبل ما شاهد تمام جرم های طالبان بودیم.همین گروپی که حکومت افغانستان را در دست دارد جرم های غیر انسانی را در مقابل مردم افغانستان انجام داده اند. همین گروه مساجد ، شفاخانه ها و مراکز آموزشی را انفجار دادند و انسانهای بی گناه را سر بریدند و اگر این گروه را به رسمیت بشناسید به یک گروه مجرم حق و رسمیت میدهید. اگر شما آنها را به رسمیت بشناسید بزرگترین ظلم را در حق دختران و زنان افغانستان انجام خواهید داد.

شگوفه شهباز

۱۴۰۲/۰۲/۱۵

# Re/calibrating

PHOTOS: TESLARIU MIHAI

Murad Khan
murad.khan@yale.edu

## Karachi, Pakistan—1997

"How many times have I said—don't put spices in the food!"

My father's voice ignited my nervous system, scorching through the oppressively humid atmosphere. My mother, who had cooked the food, stared silently at her plate.

He pointed at my eldest sister and asked, "Do you like spices?"

"No," she responded.

He pointed at my second sister and asked, "Do you like spices?"

"No," she responded.

He then pointed at me and asked, "Do you like spices?"

"Yes."

He stared back at me as if I had slapped him across the face.

"What did you say?"

"I don't mind spices."

He took me into a separate room.

"Slap yourself."

I did as I was told.

"Harder."

I increased the force.

"Harder!"

When we were done, he took me to my sisters and instructed me to share what I had learned from the evening.

I sobbed, "If Mom says go left and Dad says go right—go right."

## Karachi, Pakistan—2001

The doorbell rang.

Living in Karachi had necessitated safety routines for such situations. I went to the kitchen window and asked, "Who is it?"

"It's the postman. I have a package for you."

"Can you pass it through the grill?"

"No. It's too big. You'll have to open the door."

I checked with my mother and opened the door. I watched him step toward me, felt his arm around my shoulders, and sensed something poking at my stomach.

"If you listen to everything I say, I'll treat you all like family. No need to worry—just quietly lead me to your mother."

I realized that the object poking at my stomach was a gun. In nodding silently and leading him toward my mother, I turned right. Despite the material losses, we survived. On the way out, they warned us against filing a police report. They were "well connected" and would come after us.

A few months later, my mother came home from the police station after choosing not to identify these men despite having recognized them. As she sobbed at the same table where I had dared to say yes a few years ago, I felt the distinct urge to slap myself.

## New York City—2015

We were seated across a table from our medical school dean, months after Black students had organized a die-in expressing solidarity with Black Lives Matter, following the police murders of Michael Brown and Eric Garner. BIPOC students, particularly Black students, had been raising concerns about racism in our medical school for years. Queer students had simultaneously been raising concerns about queer- and transphobia. I was coleading what we called the Anti-Racism Coalition and representing BIPOC students with one of my Black friends.

"It's just interesting—the LGBTQ students have taken a far more collegial and collaborative approach to working with us. And look how much they have accomplished. It's different from the Anti-Racism Coalition's approach. I'm not making a value judgment—it's just an observation. You can get a lot more done if you're willing to work with us rather than seeing us as the enemy."

I stared back at him, confused, knowing that queer students were also frustrated with the administration.

"I'm queer and also work with the LGBTQ students."

"Oh," he said, seeming genuinely surprised. "I didn't realize that. I haven't seen you at those meetings."

I appreciated his honesty. I had been left out of several of these meetings. It likely didn't matter that I had been there for some of them—he still hadn't seen me. Now that he did see me, I got the impression he didn't like what he was seeing.

He was not alone.

I developed a reputation in medical school for being "disrespectful," "arrogant," "angry," "aggressive," and "militant." I was simultaneously seen as "too sensitive," "too emotional," and "too naive." I was pulled into several individual meetings and instructed to focus more on my schoolwork. When I challenged professors on oppressive material, I was reported to the administration by fellow students as creating a "hostile learning environment."

I had worked incredibly hard to leave Pakistan to pursue freedom in the United States—the freedom to choose movement in any direction with safety, love, and solidarity. After 9/11, I wasn't naive enough to think going left would be safe in airports, streets, or online. Still, experiencing the cruelty of students and faculty with access to every possible educational resource, extinguished something in me—hope. I slapped myself by going left. I endangered my loved ones and communities by going right. I had no good options left, and I did nothing right.

## New York City—2016

I chose to spend my second year in medical school sitting at the front and to the right of the podium. This position allowed me to tune out the eye-rolls and sighs that would inevitably follow if I ever dared to engage in class. In a session on physicians and human rights, the white speaker discussed physician participation in torture in Guantánamo Bay. She compared it to physician participation in anti-Semitic torture during the Holocaust. A white peer raised her hand.

"I think it's really problematic that this is being compared to the Holocaust. Unlike these prisoners, the victims of the Holocaust did nothing to deserve how they were treated."

The speaker paused. She looked around the room. She then responded, "Okay...I guess that's one opinion."

As I turned my head to face the wall on my right, class continued.

## Lahore, Pakistan—2018

"I wish we had more time. I'd really love to hold your hand."

I had returned to Pakistan for a close friend's wedding. This Pakistan was slightly different from the one I knew. I was on a date with a man I had met through Grindr.

"I'd love that too."

"I live with my family and don't have any other private, indoor spaces I can think of."

"Are there any private, outdoor spaces?"

He smiled back at me and drove to a park in a residential neighborhood. We got out and walked around in the pitch dark. Having found a bench where we thought we couldn't be seen, we sat down. He gingerly took my hand in his. While I had been out in the US for a few years, it was unlike any other tender, queer moment I had experienced.

Hardly a minute passed before he said, "I think someone's watching—we should probably go."

As we were sitting back in his car, I heard a rumble drawing closer. Two motorbikes, each carrying two men, pulled up to our left and our right. My date seemed calm.

"My friend is visiting from America," he told the police as he placed his hands behind his head. "No need to worry, Murad. Just do as they say. They're here to protect us."

They eventually left, and we got back into the car. In Pakistan, the passenger seat is on the left side of the car, so I looked to my right.

"I guess that's enough excitement for one night. Let's get you home."

## New Haven, CT—March 29, 2023

I woke up to an email from the American Psychoanalytic Association (APsA) Committee on Gender and Sexuality (CoGS) cochair, informing us that leadership had denied our request for support amid the wave of domestic and global anti-trans legislation. His email also mentioned a situation with APsA, Dr. Lara Sheehi, and the Holmes Commission on Racial Equality in American Psychoanalysis. Not having access to the APsA listserv, I was confused. Just two days prior, I had learned through another listserv that she had been cleared from an investigation for alleged anti-Semitism at George Washington University.

I met Lara briefly over Zoom in 2022, after a mentor introduced us. I had already been inspired by her courageous solidarity with oppressed groups, particularly Palestinians, and was eager to connect. I shared my anxieties about starting psychoanalytic training without having connections to BIPOC mentors. She compassionately listened, validated my experiences, and offered her support. She welcomed me to the BIPOCanalysis Collective. Witnessing the Collective mobilizing amid the allegations she was subsequently cleared from reignited something in me—hope[1]. A friend in CoGS forwarded me some of the listserv posts that summarized the situation our cochair was referring to.

I attended the following CoGS meeting, my second ever. I joined a couple of other members in expressing a desire to show solidarity with Lara and the Holmes Commission. Several expressed concerns about alienating ourselves, "inflaming" the situation, and "joining a chorus of angry voices." They wanted to focus on collaborating with leadership. I heard this as wanting to take a "collegial and collaborative approach."

Much has happened since this initial discussion. CoGS eventually pulled out of the upcoming APsA meeting and expressed solidarity with Lara and the Holmes Commission. Working through different perspectives, in this instance, CoGS eventually went left.

1 https://psychoanalyticactivist.com/2023/02/02/the-bipocanalysis-collective-statement-of-support-for-dr-lara-sheehi/

## New Haven, CT—April 16, 2023

As I continue to navigate spaces, be they within APsA or not, I am caught in discourse that is not new to me. I witness people I admire being punished for going left. I witness others' submission to and complicity in violence for going right. I confront assumptions from others that I don't know what it means to go right. Ironically, I would not be in the privileged position I am in today if I hadn't repeatedly done so. We are all caught in a three-dimensional matrix, under forces that push us in different directions depending on the context we're in at any given moment. If you disagree with another's chosen direction, I ask you to consider—maybe both of you have been pressured to go in more similar directions than you think. And maybe the consequences, for you and this other, are different for doing so—regardless of the direction you end up choosing.

## New York City—April 29, 2023

The APA Division 39 Spring Symposium was the first professional setting in which I had publicly expressed my nonbinary gender in clothing, clad with jewelry and South Asian accessories. It was raining when I stepped out of the hotel. The E train was not running, cabs weren't stopping, and Uber prices were high. I decided to walk. I placed my shawl over my head to protect myself from the rain. While I was walking south on the west side of Eighth Avenue in Hell's Kitchen, a white man passed by my left. I caught a glimpse of the expression on his face as he walked away. His rage was so striking that it took me a few seconds to realize he had shoved me into the wall—gayborhood, daylight, and passersby unperturbed. Can you guess in which direction?

**Naftally Israeli**
naftally@gmail.com



# FROM EXCLUSION TO ERASURE

I am writing this on Israel's seventy-fifth anniversary, its democratic future shrouded in fog. Sections of society that failed to gain recognition, excluded for years from the main public discourse and centers of power, are now seeking to dismantle it from within. They are enraged: they seek to use their power, this time not just to exclude others (as they themselves were excluded) but to wreak destruction and erase everything they perceived as other than them. A striving for solidarity, which was characteristic of Israel for generations, is now crumbling.

Some of that withering rage I know through personal experience. My mother's parents participated in Israel's pre-state revisionist underground and were excluded from the mainstream social, political, and professional discourse for many years.[1] To avoid being persecuted for his past, my grandfather changed his name. He and my grandmother felt their all-out effort during the foundation of the state went unacknowledged and that they and their friends were not granted the place they deserved in the new society. They were often treated with contempt, and this had repercussions, economic as well as psychological.

Two generations after that, I found myself living in a town where most of the population was Mizrahi and right-wing, unlike myself (having an Ashkenazi background). I often felt excluded and alienated there.[2] Later, I also grew aware of how outraged my Mizrahi friends felt because of the discrimination and lack of due recognition they and their parents frequently had to face.

This sentiment has been fermenting over the years, quietly murmuring below the surface. I see it unfolding on two parallel planes: social and intrapsychic. On the first, social level, rage is associated with social injustice. It is triggered whenever people do not get the recognition they expect and feel they deserve. Revisionists, Mizrahis, Ethiopian Jews,[3] women, citizens living on the periphery of Israel, Arab citizens of Israel, and, of course, Palestinians, who are deprived of human rights—all these groups and others have gone unrecognized, with the subjective experience this entails, together with a sense of not being seen. The ideas of the revisionists have been close to power for many years in Israel, but the other groups still feel they are being ignored. The experience of being ignored threatens a loss of personality, and if it goes on for too long, it is felt as contempt for the person's very existence. Axel Honneth, writing about acknowledgment, explains how in situations like this, shame and bitterness are eventually followed by rage: "The social protests of the lower classes are not motivated by positively formulated moral principles but by the experience of having their intuitive notions of justice violated. The normative core of such notions of justice is always constituted by expectations of respect for one's own dignity, honor, or integrity."[4]

Recognition, on the face of it, might be an appropriate response to this rage. But while contributing to the creation of a positive self-image, such recognition can also be leveraged as a political tool and subject individuals as well as groups to existing structures of control and power. The "obedient" slave, the "good" homemaker, the "brave" soldier, the "loyal" Mizrahi—all of these illustrate what happens when recognition seemingly elevates self-images but in fact resubjects them to power structures. For recognition to be truly ethical rather than merely ideological, it should be translated into action. What must change is the legal definitions relevant to minority groups that have gone unrecognized hitherto, different types of political representation have to be generated, and resources must be redistributed.

A new political order came into existence in Israel in the 1970s, offering what seemed to be then an acknowledgment of the rage festering among Mizrahi and revisionist citizens. As for the revisionist ideas—these are now well represented in official government policies. But while giving hope to many, this so-called political turnover did not bring about real change for other groups, because in the forty-six years of almost continuous right-wing rule since, recognition for weaker social groups (including the Mizrahis) was mainly ideological. Over the years, this kind of fake recognition only deepened the sense of disadvantage by symbolically acknowledging exclusion while not offering any material, social, or political solution.

A few corrupt Israeli politicians were, and continue to be, in charge of this process—but they are not alone. They were joined by two groups, a messianic population that seeks to further absolute Jewish supremacy, leading,

1 The revisionists were a part of the Zionist movement. Their leader was Ze'ev Jabotinsky, who wanted to establish a Jewish state in the historical land of Israel (which includes Mandatory Palestine and the nowadays state of Jordan). He was the chief competitor to David Ben-Gurion's "practical Zionism" and called to fight the British Mandate in Palestine. Revisionist Zionism strongly influenced modern right-wing Israeli parties, first Herut (led by Menachem Begin) and then its successor, Likud (led today by Benjamin Netanyahu). They were in the opposition until 1977, and from then on (except for a few years) form the coalition in Israel's government (Knesset).

2 Mizrahi Jews are a group of Jewish communities composed of those who existed in the diaspora around the Middle East and North Africa (and also those who remained in the Land of Israel). Most of these Jews came to the State of Israel in the 1950s. They were maltreated in many ways, and many of them felt disrespected by the other Jewish groups in Israel, especially the Ashkenazi (those who immigrated from Europe during the first half of the 20th century, took part in the establishment of the State of Israel, and many of them were holding key positions in the government and in other social institutes). Menachem Begin, as head of the opposition for many years, called for inclusion of the Mizrahi in the formal and informal institutions in Israel.

3 Ethiopian Jews are a Jewish community that lived for centuries in Ethiopia. Most of them immigrated to Israel in the 1990s. Different in skin color and in culture, they are often misunderstood, suffer from discrimination in many areas, and are maltreated in many ways.

4 Axel Honneth, *Disrespect: The Normative Foundations of Critical Theory* (Cambridge: Polity Press, 2007), 71.

to all intents and purposes, to an apartheid regime, first and foremost in the occupied territories, but beyond that, throughout Israel; and an ultra-Orthodox section (including only a small proportion of the country's ultra-Orthodox [Haredi] citizens and mainly consisting of its political leadership), which acts to maintain itself—its children deprived of a modern education and its women going without representation in their communities—sealed off from the rest of Israeli society.[5] Having entered a destructive pact, these politicians, aided by these two extremely ideological groups, are now acting like a parasitic element, threatening to crush Israel's social contract and solidarity. This pact perversely leads from exclusion to erasure in a process I believe Donald Meltzer[6], the psychoanalyst, has well described. His psychoanalytic explanation describes the perverse person's tendency to give up on truth in order to maintain control and power by means of the other's erasure.

From an intrapsychic perspective, perversion emerges from the personality's evil, infantile part, when it experiences envious rivalry toward idealized objects. It fans omnipotent situations, which it then grounds in the real world by means of confusing inner and outer reality. In its social version, one part of society takes a parasitic position in relation to the others. The corrupt politicians and the leaders of the other two groups I described use mental tools grounded in splitting, projection, and incitement to take destructive action. The attendant effect is fundamentally manic, feeding upon a sense of power: I can do whatever I like, and more specifically: I can do whatever I like to the other. The underlying method is to single out the other and then unleash aggression upon them, to sow confusion and weaken the truth so as to set the scene for casting this other as the source of evil. Fake news, therefore, is currently in massive circulation in Israel, as well as a groundswell of populism and attacks on the basic distinction between good and evil. That's the world of Orwell's 1984, in which it is all but impossible to tell truth from lie, good from bad. That's the world whose picture the prophet Isaiah sketches: "[...] those that call evil good, and good evil; that put darkness for light, and light for darkness" (Isaiah 5:20). In a world like this, in Israel today, the problem is not the many lies we are being fed. It is obvious that our politicians are telling lies. The problem is that from the sheer amount of lies, it has become hard to make out the truth even when it is staring us right in the eye. The resulting distress, anxiety, and frustration cause many to look for a source of comfort and security—which they find among exactly the same politicians who knowingly deceive them.

What can be said about this destructive pact that is currently leading Israel into disaster is that in the long run, a complex and integrated view of the truth cannot be maintained while simultaneously excluding entire swaths of the population from ethical (not just ideological) recognition. The corrupt politicians and the leaders of the two extremist groups fear that when their lies falter, they will lose their ability to control, so they know the only way to continue victimizing their followers is by deepening the lies they are telling them. The corrupt leadership knows this about the Mizrahis'—and other social groups'—sense of disadvantage. The leaders of the messianic Israelis know this about the Palestinians, who are bereft of basic human rights. The Haredi leadership knows this about its offspring: not all of them think the same, and many would like to get an education, serve in the army, and become part of Zionist society. In order to preserve their pact, the leaders of these groups and our corrupt politicians believe they have no choice but to turn exclusion into erasure, which comes at the price of truth. In other words: they choose the way of perversion.

Many of us, appalled at the terrible truth, cannot believe it. Such destruction has been wreaked here in the past few months in the name of preserving their destructive pact, and at what speed has it been achieved! Soldiers who have fought for their country have been called "anarchists," and a government minister has told them to "go to hell"; leaders who dedicated their whole life to their homeland have been called "traitors." A government minister has called "to wipe out" a Palestinian village while the prime minister does not denounce severe social violence, not even when it occurs in cemeteries, during Israel's annual commemoration for Israel's fallen soldiers.

For the sake of the future, will we manage to stop these powers? As we are now facing apparent madness in Israel, will we find a leader who can take us back on the path of sanity and truth? Are there brave leaders among us who can guide us back from the path of perversion in order to choose, instead, solidarity, help us restore our democratic future, and save our children from perdition? ■

*Special thank you to Mirjam Meerschwam Hadar for help with the translation.*

5 The ultra-Orthodox Jews and the Messianic groups are both very religious groups, but they differ in their nationalistic orientation. The Messianic group consists mainly of Jews living in the occupied territories and having an ideology of nationalism and Jewish supremacy. The ultra-Orthodox live in closed communities everywhere in Israel, and their leaders practice politics mainly in order to preserve (by way of receiving governmental money and by legislating laws) their very extreme way of life (not studying mathematics or English in their schools, their women having no representational rights, their men studying the Jewish holy scripts for most of their life and not working, and so on).

6 Donald Meltzer, *Sexual States of Mind* (Clunie Press, Perthshire, 1973).

חלק קטן מהחרדים ובעיקר את מנהיגיהם הפוליטיים), שפועלת כדי לשמור על עצמה סגורה בפני קבוצות אחרות בישראל, על ילדיה חסרי השכלה מודרנית ועל נשיה חסרות ייצוג במוסדות הקהילה. ברית הנאמנות ההרסנית בין שתי קבוצות אלה ובין הפוליטיקאים המושחתים פועלת כגורם טפילי, שמאיים להרוס את הסולידריות החברתית הישראלית. ברית הנאמנות הזאת מובילה מהדרה למחיקה, בדרך פרוורטית שהייטיב לתארה בעיניי הפסיכואנליטיקאי **דונלד מלצר** (1973)[2]. ההסבר הפסיכואנליטי שלו מדגיש את הנטייה של הפרוורטי לוותר על האמת כדי לשמור על שליטה וכוח באמצעות מחיקה של האחר.

מנקודת מבט תוך-אישית, יסודה של הפרוורסיה הוא בחלק הילדי הרע של האישיות, שמרגיש תחרותיות צרת עין כלפי אובייקטים מואדרים. הוא מלבה מצבים של כל-יכולות (אומניפוטנציה), ועל ידי בלבול בין מציאות פנימית וחיצונית מבסס אותם גם בעולם החיצוני. בגרסה החברתית, מדובר בחלק של החברה שמתנהג באופן טפילי כלפי החברה כולה. מנהיגי שתי הקבוצות שתיארתי, ביחד עם הפוליטיקאים המושחתים, מפעילים כלים מנטליים לפעולות הרסניות, שיסודן בפיצול, השלכה והסתה. האיכות הרגשית היא מאנית ביסודה, ומקורה בתחושת כוח: אני יכול לעשות מה שמתחשק לי, ובאופן ספציפי יותר: אני יכול לעשות **לאַחֵר** מה שמתחשק לי. השיטה הבסיסית היא לתייג את "האחר", ואז לשסות בו את הכוחות התוקפניים; ליצור בלבול וכך להחליש את האמת ולהכשיר את הקרקע לתפיסת אותו "אחר" כמקור הרוע. לשם כך, בישראל של היום יש שימוש מסיבי בפייק ניוז, בפופוליזם ובהתקפה על ההבחנה בין טוב ורע. זה העולם של "1984" של ג'ורג' אורוול, שבו קשה עד בלתי אפשרי להבחין בין אמת ושקר, טוב ורע. זהו העולם שמשרטט הנביא ישעיהו: "האומרים לרע טוב ולטוב רע, שמים חושך לאור ואור לחושך" (ישעיהו פרק ה פסוק 20). בעולם כזה, בישראל של היום, הבעיה היא לא השקרים הרבים שמספרים לנו. ברור שהפוליטיקאים שלנו משקרים. הבעיה היא שמרוב שקרים כבר קשה להבחין באמת כשהיא מול עינינו ממש. המצוקה, החרדה וחוסר האונים שהמצב הזה יוצר מובילים אנשים רבים לחפש מקור לנחמה ולביטחון, והם מוצאים אותו בידיהם של אותם פוליטיקאים שמשקרים להם ביודעין ובכוונה.

המשותף לפוליטיקאים המושחתים ולמנהיגי הקבוצות שמובילים היום את ישראל לחורבן היא ההבנה שלאורך זמן אי אפשר להחזיק בראייה מורכבת ואינטגרטיבית של האמת ובו-זמנית להדיר חלקים שלמים מהאוכלוסיה בלי לתת להם הכרה מוסרית (ולא רק אידיאולוגית). הם פוחדים שכאשר יתגלו השקרים שלהם, הם יאבדו את היכולת לשלוט, ולכן הם יודעים שהדרך היחידה להמשיך ולקרבן את נאמניהם היא באמצעות העמקת השקרים שהם מספרים להם. הפוליטיקאים המושחתים יודעים שכך הדבר לגבי תחושת הקיפוח של המזרחים ושל קבוצות אחרות באוכלוסיה. המנהיגים המשיחיים יודעים שכך הדבר כלפי הפלסטינים, שנעדרים כבר היום זכויות אדם בסיסיות. ההנהגה החרדית יודעת שכך הדבר כלפי בניה שלה, שאינם "מקשה אחת" ורבים מהם רוצים להשכיל, לשרת ולהשתלב בחברה הציונית. כדי להמשיך בברית הנאמנות שכרתו קבוצות אלה "אין להן ברירה" אלא להפוך הדרה למחיקה, והמחיר הוא ויתור על האמת, כלומר בחירה בדרך הפרוורטית.

רבים כמוני עומדים כלא מאמינים, משתאים מול האמת הנוראה: כמה הרס נזרע כאן בחודשים האחרונים בשם המטרה הזאת, ובאיזה קצב מהיר אפשר להשיגו! חיילים שלחמו למען המדינה מכונים "אנרכיסטים" ושר בממשלה קורא "שֶׁיֵּלְכוּ לעזאזל"; מנהיגים שנתנו את כל חייהם לשירות הציבורי מכונים "בוגדים". שר בממשלה קורא למחוק כפר פלסטיני וראש הממשלה אינו מגנה אלימות חברתית קשה, אפילו בתוך בתי קברות ביום הזיכרון לחללי מערכות ישראל.

האם נצליח לעצור את כוחות ההרס האלה, למען העתיד? בימים כאלה אני חושב על מאמרו של היינץ קוהוט, "Introspection, empathy and the semi-circle of mental health" (1982)[3]. קוהוט נזכר שם באודיסיאוס, שכדי לשמור על חייו ולהימנע מגיוס למלחמה (למען אשתו ובנו שאך נולד), עשה עצמו כמשוגע: הוא זרע את שדהו במלח ורתם שור וחמור יחדיו למחרשה. פלאמדס חשד בו. הוא אחז בטלמכוס, בנו של אודיסאוס, וזרק אותו לרגלי המחרשה. אודיסיאוס הטה מייד את המחרשה והוביל אותה לאורך חצי מעגל (semi-circle), מסביב לטלמכוס. בכך הוא הוכיח את שפיותו ואת דחף החיים הבריא שלו; מול ההכרח לבחור בין שפיות ושיגעון הוא פעל מייד להצלת בנו, להצלת העתיד. בְּעָמְדֵנוּ היום בישראל מול מה שנראה כשיגעון, האם יימצא לנו מנהיג כמו אודיסיאוס? האם יימצא לנו מנהיג שיצליח להחזיר אותנו לדרך השפיות והאמת? האם יש בינינו מנהיגים אמיצים שמסוגלים לנווט את המדינה שלנו בחזרה מהדרך הפרוורטית ולבחור בסולידריות, להחזיר לנו בחזרה את עתידנו הדמוקרטי ולהציל את ילדינו מאבדון?

---

[2] מלצר, דונלד (2021). מצבי נפש מיניים (ישראל, תולעת ספרים).

[3] Kohut, H. (1982). Introspection, empathy, and the semi-circle of mental health. *The International Journal of Psychoanalysis*, 63(4), 395–407.

# מהדרה למחיקה

מספרים שקשה היה לסמוך על התנהגותה של אריס, אלת הריב והמדון. לחתונה של פליאוס ותטיס, בתו של אל הים פוסידון, שנערכה על האולימפוס, הוזמנו כל האלים חוץ ממנה. אריס כעסה והחליטה לנקום. היא גנבה תפוח מגן העדן של ההספרידות (בנותיו של הלילה), תפוח מזהב טהור, כתבה עליו "ליפה ביותר" וגלגלה אותו לרגליהן של שלוש האלות החזקות באולימפוס: הרה (אשתו של זאוס, אבי האלים), אתנה (אלת החכמה) ואפרודיטה (אלת האהבה). כל אחת מהשלוש חשבה שהתפוח מיועד לה, ומי שנבחר לפסוק ביניהן היה פריס, בנו האבוד של פריאמוס, מלך טרויה. כך החל "משפט פריס", ובסופו פסק פריס שאפרודיטה היא היפה ביותר. הרה ואתנה זעמו. הן עזרו לבני ספרטה לפלוש לטרויה ולהרוס אותה, וכך ניצתה מלחמה אכזרית שבה נפלו רבים מגיבורי יוון.

אני כותב את הדברים האלה ביום העצמאות ה-75 של מדינת ישראל, כשעתידה הדמוקרטי לוט בערפל. קבוצות בחברה הישראלית, שלא קיבלו הכרה ובמשך שנים הודרו מהשיח וממוקדי הכוח מבקשות כעת לפרק אותה מבפנים. כמו אריס, הן זועמות, ומבקשות להשתמש בכוחן והפעם לא רק כדי להדיר אחרים (כפי שהדירו אותן) אלא גם כדי לנקום, לזרוע הרס ולמחוק את כל מה שנתפס כשונה מהן. הסולידריות, דהיינו ה"דבק" החברתי שאפיין את החברה הישראלית במשך דורות, מתפוררת.

חלק מהזעם המפורר הזה מוכר לי באופן אישי. הוריה של אמי פעלו במחתרות הרביזיוניסטיות, ובמשך שנים הודרו מהזרם המרכזי בישראל - החברתי, הפוליטי והמקצועי. כדי לא להיות רדוף על ידי עברו, סבי החליט לשנות את שם משפחתו. הוא וסבתי הרגישו שלא מכירים בפועלם הנחוש למען הקמת המדינה, ולא נותנים להם ולחבריהם את המקום הראוי בה. במקומות רבים הפנו להם עורף, והיו לכך כמובן גם השפעות כלכליות ונפשיות. שני דורות לאחר מכן, כילד מבית אשכנזי חוויתי על בשרי את ההדרה ואת הזרות ביישוב שגדלתי בו, שהרוב בו היה אחר ממני - ימני ומזרחי. לימים, הכרתי מקרוב גם את הזעם של חלק מחבריי המזרחים, זעם על היעדר ההכרה באפליה שהם והוריהם סבלו ממנה.

הזעם הזה טופח במשך שנים, והוא רוחש מתחת לפני השטח. אני רואה אותו פועל בשני מישורים במקביל: חברתי ותוך-נפשי. במישור החברתי הזעם הזה קשור לאירועים של אי צדק: אירועים שבהם נשללה מאנשים, בניגוד לציפיותיהם, ההכרה שלדעתם הם ראויים לה. רביזיוניסטים, מזרחים, אתיופים, נשים, תושבי הפריפריה, ערבים אזרחי ישראל וכמובן הפלסטינים משוללי זכויות האזרח - כל הקבוצות האלה, ואחרות, מרגישות משוללות הכרה, והחוויה הסובייקטיבית הנלווית לכך היא תחושה של התעלמות, תחושה של חוסר נראות. החוויה של התעלמות היא איום באובדן האישיות, ואם הוא נמשך זמן רב מדי הוא נחווה כזלזול בעצם הקיום של האדם. **אקסל הונת**, שכתב על מתן הכרה, מסביר שאחרי הבושה ותחושת המרמור מגיע הזעם: "הכוח המניע את המחאה החברתית של השכבות הנמוכות אינם עקרונות מוסריים המנוסחים באופן פוזיטיבי, אלא חוויית הפגיעה בדימויים אינטואיטיביים של צדק; ובליבה הנורמטיבית של דימויי צדק אלה נמצאות תמיד ציפיותיו של האדם לקבל הכרה בערכו, בכבודו או ביושרתו" (עמ' 50, 2008).[1]

מתן הכרה היה יכול לתת מענה לזעם הזה, לכאורה. אולם מתן הכרה, שתורם ליצירת דימוי עצמי חיובי, יכול להיות כלי שרת פוליטי, ולהכפיף יחידים וקבוצות למבנים קיימים של שליטה. העבד ה"צייתן", עקרת הבית ה"טובה", החייל ה"גיבור", המזרחי ה"נאמן" - כל אלה דוגמות למתן הכרה שכביכול מרומם את הדימוי העצמי של האדם אך למעשה משעבד אותו בחזרה לתוך מנגנוני שליטה קיימים. כדי שמתן הכרה יהיה באמת מוסרי ואנושי, ולא רק אידיאולוגי, הוא צריך להיות מתורגם למעשים: חייבות להשתנות הגדרות משפטיות הנוגעות לקבוצות מיעוטים שלא קיבלו עד היום הכרה, חייבות להתכונן צורות אחרות של ייצוג פוליטי, וחייבת להתבצע חלוקה מחדש של המשאבים.

בישראל כונן ייצוג פוליטי חדש בסוף שנות השבעים של המאה ה-20, והייצוג הזה נתן אז הכרה מסוימת לזעם שהצטבר בקרב הרביזיוניסטים והמזרחים. היום הרעיונות הרביזיוניסטיים מיוצגים היטב במדיניות הממשלתית הרשמית. אבל ה"מהפך" של 1977, שנתן תקווה לרבים, לא הצליח להניע תהליכי שינוי אמיתיים משום שמאז - במשך 46 שנים של שלטון ימני כמעט רציף - מתן ההכרה לקבוצות המוחלשות (כולל המזרחים) היה אידיאולוגי בעיקרו. לאורך שנים מתן הכרה כזה רק טיפח והעמיק עוד ועוד את תחושת הקיפוח, משום שהוא אמנם הכיר באופן סמלי בהדרה אבל לא נתן לה מענה חומרי, חברתי ופוליטי.

כמה פוליטיקאים מושחתים הובילו וממשיכים להוביל את המהלך הזה בישראל, אבל הם לא לבד. חברו להם שתי קבוצות: קבוצה משיחית, שרוצה להחיל את העליונות היהודית באופן מוחלט ולכונן הלכה למעשה שלטון אפרטהייד, בראש ובראשונה בשטחים הכבושים ולאחר מכן בישראל כולה; וקבוצה חרדית (שכוללת

[1] הונת, אקסל (2008). זלזול ומתן הכרה: לקראת תיאוריה ביקורתית חדשה (תל-אביב, הקיבוץ המאוחד).

**Matt A. Hanson**
mhanson1717@yahoo.com



# Adventures in Turkish Journalism

## SESSION I

I had reached a new low. The heights of the literary profession had never seemed more distant, unreachable. In fact, I lived in an attic. It was a hot and unbearable Istanbul summer. I woke every morning and sometimes every afternoon caked in sweat under the wooden roof on the top floor of a residential building in the modernistic environs of Besiktas, a neighborhood synonymous with football, beer, and anarchy.

I was living rent-free with my girlfriend from Ankara, in the home of her aunt and uncle, the artistic director of a modern dance company funded by the corrupt state and an English rock star, respectively—not the most typical of Turkish families.

I tried to meditate, drink, smoke, and pray my anxieties away. It worked only when my eyes were firmly shut. When I opened them, I scanned my empty inbox.

I had sent unreturned pitches to every newspaper and magazine under the burning sun since first arriving in Turkey the winter before, green from Brooklyn, wearing my heart on my sleeve.

I pitched desperately, like a bad poet. I was striking out. The game was not over. It felt like it would never begin.

## SESSION II

I heard back about a story. I would explore a survey of expatriate literature for a shamelessly pro-government, B-film equivalent of a newspaper, the head of state's new international media pet project, an English-language Turkish broadsheet infamous for its bigoted corporate policy, its far-right propagandizing, its bastardized, sixth-grade-level English, left sorely unedited and wildly inaccurate.

The fear and loathing of its frequently infantile language are only surpassed by the publication's chief mandate: censorship. Its very institution is that of obscuring facts in the name of strongman authoritarianism. They often block stories outright, in the style of Turkish media's routine media blackouts, all in the face of even its most loyal and perfunctorily celebrated in-house writers.

Without the slightest trace of editorial integrity, its editors do not edit. They censor and employ subordinates to pay thoughtless, uncritical lip service to the incarcerating doublespeak of the political overhaul that came after the 2016 coup attempt.

The paper has a long blacklist of names, which includes everyone from the country's most famous national writer, Orhan Pamuk, to those as benign as the geologist Celâl Şengör. In a variety of passive-aggressive gestures, its team of censors assumes the guise of editors, defending asinine, anachronistic, homophobic bigotries as "corporate policy."

Referring to alcohol, drugs, sex, and even revealing factual aspects of Turkey's multiethnic history in mere culture writing is a liability known to cost jobs. And there is no fact-checking department.

It is truly a post-apocalyptic form of media. Imagine reportage from a world barely inhabited after a global collapse. Muted by a lingering, doomsday climate of political fear, civic space has been overshadowed by the blockage of free assembly and the silencing of free speech. The public, like its publications, is confined to mere commerce, mediation between private holdings, and a kind of state-chaperoned revelry.

But I had to work and could not afford to uphold my political conscience. I traded my pride for a reprieve from total financial dependency, from the dire straits of the inexperienced foreign correspondence freelancer with no independent wealth to my name whatsoever. I was rooted in a modest upbringing, as the class-conscious grandson of immigrant New Yorkers up from the Jewish sweatshop, raised by the nobility of multigenerational workers.

## SESSION III

I was and remain a radical leftist, committed to a world that secures universal rights and gender equity, freedom of expression and social justice, oppositional pluralism and wealth distribution, religious tolerance and ecological rights, indigenous resistance and internationalist solidarity, creative sustainability and cultural diversity.

One day I walked into the swanky Pera Palace Hotel, following in the footsteps of Agatha Christie and Papa Hemingway, John Dos Passos and Knut Hamsun, to meet the American novelist and veteran Elliot Ackerman.

He was a decorated combat veteran, having served five tours of duty in Iraq and Afghanistan. He had worked in the White House. He met with a member of Al-Qaeda in the city of Gaziantep, the embattled Turkish east at the doorway to Syria, and wrote about it rivetingly.

When asked about his recent piece for *The New Yorker* covering the June 2016 attack at Ataturk Airport, among epic political histories profiling Turkey's President Erdoğan, he downplayed the prestige of the magazine that is the pinnacle of literary success for most people, including me. He said he was a novelist foremost. His publisher Knopf sent me a proof of his second novel, *Dark at the Crossing*, which became a finalist for the National Book Award.

I remembered what Hemingway said to writers about journalism, himself a seasoned war reporter on the fronts of the Spanish Civil War, witnessing the plight of refugees in Thrace during the 1923 Population Exchange between Greece and Turkey. It is good experience at first, he warned, but not for long. It is easy to get mixed up in it and forget the true art and honesty of the craft of writing itself.

## SESSION IV

I soon moved to a "village on the Bosphorus" on the Asian side of Istanbul in an out-of-the-way district and continued to send freelance pitches. In the meantime, I drafted a travelogue after an excursion to Greece, with photo essays and oral history interviews to research a novel that I had planned to write long before moving to Istanbul.

I lived cheaply and sublet my rental in Brooklyn for side income and wrote for boutique magazines with names like *Kinfolk*, *212*, *The Carton*, *Tohu*, or *Art Unlimited*, but mostly there were stories I wanted to do that no one would take.

I researched the world of post-Ottoman interfaith society in my neighborhood, with its church, synagogue, and mosque charmingly side by side across from a tea garden under a plane tree at the shorefront park. The culture section of the pro-government rag ate it up.

I held out for another year, pitching and pitching, exasperated, unanswered. Finally, I caved. I asked to become a regular contributing writer to the newspaper that represented everything that was wrong with Turkey and much of the world. They accepted. I would produce two stories a week.

## FINAL SESSION

For the next five years I did not miss one week. I also started writing for many of the most widely read art magazines in the world. After I critiqued the newspaper I was working for in a piece for the International Center for Journalists, they let me go. I could only surmise the coincidence.

I let go, too, not only of an outlet to write for (and importantly, to be paid for writing) but of my constant self-loathing. I was not proud of working for them. I was not being true to my soul.

Colleagues at *The New York Times* and *The Nation* encouraged me all along. But it is only now, when I look back and meet with complimentary readers from my field, that I realize the benefits of having stepped outside my comfort zone.

People were not only amused and enlightened by my pieces for that newspaper. I was an individual with a voice, crying out among the unheard, struggling to write about contemporary art in Turkey as a matter of free expression. I did my time.

Now, untethered from the incorporation of government censorship, I am working harder than ever toward an end that I have never cared less to define. My path and I are part of one organic, mystifying presence of interdependent wholeness with the natural world. And when I rest, my dreams rise and fall. ■

**Destiney Kirby**
destiney.kirby@einsteinmed.edu

# On Hair Care

Every day, I have engaged in the sacred ritual that is my hair care. I gently mist my coily strands with water, apply a cream filled with the building blocks of life, and seal with an oil scented by the gods in heaven itself. This daily tradition has become a point of pride, a coat of arms tying me to the ancestral roots of struggle and resilience. It was not always this way.

My hair could have been held in court as evidence of child neglect. My birth was preceded by an endless list of questions concerning paternity, but the dark, coarse corkscrews that sprang from my crown only served to lengthen the list. My mother's loose auburn curls explained half my head, but the other half remained unaccounted for. My family would later joke, "We didn't know whose you were, but we knew you weren't white."

As I grew older, my mother would experience significant difficulty managing my hair without the help of the internet to direct her. She would succumb to four-hundred-degree flat irons in between long treks from our rural home to the Black hair salons in the city. I could imagine the pride she must have swallowed as she, a white woman from the country, toted a brown baby with a lion's mane to a space where she was met only with judgmental eyes. She would drop me off at the front and explain to the stylists that I needed a chemical relaxer and press. A "relaxer" was a cream that could be applied to textured hair, effectively breaking its structure and allowing the hair to hang straight until the new, curly growth came in months later.

I remember their scoffs at the white woman who demanded her Black child be rid of something so inherent to her culture. My mother would insist that she had errands to run and would leave for three or four hours at a time. We did not have family or friends on that side of the river; nor did I ever see the groceries and envelopes that came from our other errand runs. Looking back, my heart aches to think that she may not have had errands but more likely needed a reason to leave the critical onlookers. At the same time, I believe their criticism was warranted and necessary.

In the salon, the stylists treated me like their own daughters and insisted I show respect with "yes, ma'am" and "no, ma'am." My newfound aunties asked about school, sports, and gossip among my friends. They were impressed with my straight As and the number of books I could read. They loved that I was athletically talented and would tease that the boys would have difficulty keeping up with me. The salon was my first witnessing of the phrase "Black excellence."

The stylists would ask, "Are you sure you want a relaxer? You want your hair to be bone straight? We could keep a bit of texture in it." I wanted so badly to have the perfectly straight hair of my family members and classmates. Their fine-textured hair, light blue eyes, fair skin, and angular noses were the standard of beauty that I found myself both suffocating in and never getting enough of. It was my first high.

Stronger than my desire to look exactly like those around me, however, was my desire to please others. Hesitantly, I would reply, "Whatever you think will look good."

"Yeah, let's keep a little texture in it," the stylists would insist every time, without fail. As an eight-year-old child struggling with the budding self-hatred of internalized racism, I detested this. I wanted the chemicals to strip away every ounce of Blackness they could find so I could finally be considered *beautiful*. As an adult who now holds an immense amount of pride in my Black heritage, I am grateful for their insistence. My aunties forced me to drown in the spirit of our community until I was finally able to see it for all its glory.

The chemicals burned my skin, breaking the bonds of my hair so the stylists could reshape it into something I felt was more acceptable. I sat in the padded chairs, head on fire, until the flames were ready to be put out.

In between these long salon days, I was tasked with taking care of my own hair. I tried my best to brush, oil, and wrap as the ladies in the salon had taught me, but my small, uncoordinated hands could never re-create their masterpiece. I grew frustrated as my coils transformed into foul-smelling mats, which I would regretfully attempt to hide from classmates and teachers.

Again, my hair could have been held in court as evidence of child neglect. I could see photos of the carpet rug my head had mutated into projected onto a big screen for the judge and jury. This was followed by evidence of our dirty house, filled with cigarette smoke, mice, and moldy piles of dishes. I cried in my bathroom, pulling harder and harder at the strands, adding more oil between attempts. The pain meant nothing if I could somehow brush my hair into the silky threads of my white family and friends. Nothing mattered if I could believe I was beautiful. After hours of tears, I would collapse into a heap on the wool-covered floor, hating the body I was born into.

This cycle continued throughout my childhood until I finally gave up. It was exhausting and expensive. I was tired of burning myself for the approval of others. I was lucky that the internet and the subsequent Natural Hair Movement had started to grow as I progressed into my teen years. Late nights of web surfing led me to forums of other Black women, who, too, had grown tired of the constant self-hatred. I read about conspiracies of ancient queens in Africa whose mummies had evidence of scarring from the hair chemicals we continued to use in the present. I found pictures of women who had reclaimed their identities, boldly shaving their heads bald and allowing the chaos of our beautiful Black hair to slowly take over like a garden blooming in the late spring.

I had never seen women celebrated for their brown skin and wild hair. I was filled with such envy.

"But what are you going to do with it after you cut the ends? Won't it look crazy?" my grandmother, and best friend at the time, asked my fifteen-year-old self after I explained the multi-year-long plan. I had chosen to transition my hair rather than shaving it off. I would grow out my natural, virgin hair while keeping the frail but straight ends attached, styling it so it would be less noticeable.

I held close to a strict regimen that would protect my hair while it was growing. I used the hidden money under my bed to travel to beauty supply stores on the other side of town, paying for hair products that my family had never heard of. I spent hours in the night frantically reading, foaming at the mouth, to gain any piece of information I could get my hands on. The days seemed to stretch into an eternity as my coily hair grew one-quarter of an inch each month. I grew my hair for two years, abstaining from any heat or chemicals, until I was ready to put it all behind me.

That day, I dug my hands into the thick tropical-scented cream and applied it to my heat-damaged ends one last time. Section by section, I slowly and deliberately detangled the strands with a wide-toothed comb. I wanted to lay a perfect foundation for what was to come, taking immense caution with every pull of the comb. I rinsed the cream out with lukewarm water, just as my aunties on the internet had taught me. I stared at myself in the mirror, seeing two truths at once looking back. I saw the part of myself that was deeply aching for love and acceptance: the years of struggling, telling myself that "beauty is pain" and what I should strive for most. I also saw a future of new beginnings, discomfort, and growth: a future filled with acceptance and discovery.

The next hour was spent slowly trimming away every strand of chemically relaxed hair I could find. Each clip of the scissors was another day of self-hatred shed from my aching shoulders.

I stared into the reflection of my tear-filled almond eyes, as dark as the night.

She stared back.

"It's nice to meet you." ■

*Conversations with my dad 2*
*Encaustics on wood panel*
*46" X 32"*
*2023*

## Reuben Sinha

reubensinha.com



Traversing boundaries, cultures gained and cultures lost, and sensations across time and space are continual themes in my work. I left India at age eight and, ever since, have worked to reconcile what has been lost and found. My work is a continual meditation on memory and the body using line, color and form. Each work begins with raw materials: wood panels cut from prefabricated doors, beeswax from local farms, damar crystals and basic color pigments. In natural light, these paintings carry a translucency created by pigments suspended in beeswax, evoking sensuousness, depth, and personal reflection. In 2018, I began a series of brown encaustic color studies to explore the limits of a single color's expression. The series is a response to mass disenfranchisement under Trump and growing xenophobia against brown skin. To some, brown is beautiful. To others, it is dirty; the outsider, the enemy. These color studies mirror the skin of the NYC public school students I teach. By layering and blending loving and hateful associations to "Brown," I have developed a personal meditation on Otherness. These meditations on "Brown" have naturally incorporated expressions of isolation, anxiety, and calm emerging from the COVID-19 pandemic.

*Conversations with my dad 1*
*Encaustics on wood panel*
*41" X 36"*
*2023*

*Conversations with my dad 6*
*Encaustics on wood panel*
*40" X 34"*
*2023*

*Conversations with my dad 3*
*Encaustics on wood panel*
*2.5" x 28"*
*2023*

*Conversations with my dad 4*
*Encaustics on wood panel*
*36" X 27"*
*2023*

**Catherine Baker-Pitts**
drbakerpitts@gmail.com



# RAPE ON TRIAL

I spent the better part of a month in 2022 in lower Manhattan on a wooden bench in the back of a courtroom, observing a rape trial. Early on, I'd concluded my testimony on behalf of the victim, but, emotionally invested and unable to shift my attention, I kept showing up. The plaintiff had sought psychotherapy with me in 2017 to address symptoms of anxiety and body loathing. In an initial session, I asked if she had ever experienced unwanted sexual contact. "Yes, that happened," she told me in a forthright and detached manner. Like most victims who do not readily label their experiences as rape, she tried for years to put it behind her. That changed a few months into our work, when her assailant, a public figure, publicly condemned Harvey Weinstein. She was jolted by his hypocrisy amid the watershed #metoo movement.

Many people can recall when they first heard the hashtag #metoo. On October 16, 2017, one of my sisters penned on Facebook simply: "#metoo: 35 years to life worth"—the prison term the man who raped her is serving. Statistically, one in four women is likely to be sexually assaulted. Between my three sisters and me, we have survived not only a serial rapist but child molestation by a babysitter, a group assault in a country far from home that also warranted legal wrangling and a settlement, date rapes that wouldn't be named, and an attack from behind in broad daylight by a stranger in a baseball cap who didn't count on blood-curdling screams. These are only the most egregious incidents—like the 63 percent of sexual violations that go unreported, most of the gropes and intrusions we've endured are barely acknowledged even to ourselves. In her anthology *Not That Bad*, Roxane Gay asks, "What is it like to live in a culture where it often seems like it is a question of when, not if, a woman will encounter some kind of sexual violence?"

Many of us concede that our bodies are not fully ours to own. In therapy spaces and in private contemplation, we grapple with this basic betrayal: our bodies are exploited by consumer capitalism, by the male gaze, by conservative courts, and by medical model treatments that—among so many fundamental blind spots—aggressively misgender trans people, stigmatize fat people, and require us all to submit to normative codes of gender, health, and embodiment. This conditioning, of course, dissuades vulnerable people from calling out wrongful, even harmful, treatment. Some of us end up hypervigilant, on high alert for danger. Others might feel alienated, insecure, and mistrustful of our own bodies.

Even outside social media, though, pockets of resistance inspire us in our collective unconscious. The Bolivian Mennonite women (fictionalized in Sarah Polley's adaptation of Miriam Toews' *Women Talking*) who were routinely drugged, assaulted, and bloodied violated community codes and began talking about the violence that is rape. They had been denied education and literacy, but they understood that the sexual violence posed a humanitarian crisis. It was not in their "wild female imagination"; it was not isolated, and no one asked for it. Refusing to pass complicity on to their children, they actively debated whether to do nothing, to stay and fight, or to flee. Ultimately, they could not reimagine the colony beyond a state of violence, so they piled into their buggies and left their fathers, husbands, brothers, and sons of a certain age behind. In a remote dwelling with its own rules, the female-identified Mennonite people reckoned, collective denial was no longer tenable. Rape is not the individual's burden to carry.

My sisters and I knew intellectually that none of it was our fault, thanks to the groundwork laid by feminists and other women at wits' end before us. Canaries in the coal mine, feminists of the 1960s, like my mother, named the entwined problems of domestic dependency and violence in homes. Yet their disruptive ideas about sexual freedom, affirmative consent, and reproductive rights in the public sphere were generally dismissed as shrill, man-hating views of a loud minority. It was a time when women did not have the capital to speak up without being blamed, stigmatized, and punished.

I returned to that courtroom again and again after my time on the witness stand because I needed to know if anything had changed. Did the legal system reflect the inroads made by agitators before us and by the more recent movement of survivors' collective action and truth-telling?

I witnessed the awesome power of women speaking up—one after the next, victims in addition to the plaintiff provided testimony demonstrating a pattern of predatory behavior. These women created a counternarrative to the shame, self-doubt, and silence that deepen the trauma of rape.

But another thing happened. Strikingly, the strategies of legal defense relied on retrograde rape myths. These struck me as performance pieces, white-knuckled clutches on a bygone era of sexual domination that relied on gaslighting, victim blaming, and slut shaming. Old-fashioned and pathetic, the defense's counterattacks presumed the jurors to be unsophisticated about misogyny, unsympathetic to psychological truth-telling, and unknowing about the complicated face of trauma.

The defense team concocted a far-fetched fantasy about the victim feeling rejected, calling it rape, and seeking revenge. They demanded, why didn't she go to the police after she was assaulted? As expert witness Dr. Lisa Rocchio testified, rape is the most underreported crime. Only 21 percent of victims report it. More than twenty women were assaulted by Weinstein before Filipino-Italian model Ambra Gutierrez first reported the crime. It was little mystery to me why women retreat to silence when, on the stand, my former patient was interrogated about every sexual encounter she'd ever had. She was instructed to reenact the body position and movements of the assault, to remember in her body what she had tried to forget. (The cruelty on display, and her uncontrollable sobbing, brought the courtroom to an early halt that day.)

The aggressive lashes by the enfeebled defense continued. If the plaintiff felt scared that night, the defense demanded, why didn't she look for a weapon or kick her rapist? The defendant admitted that she had told him "no" and "stop" repeatedly; he described how she resisted his removal of her tights, pulling them up as he was yanking them down. Somehow, he interpreted this as an invitation. According to her rapist, "She did not say no in the way one means no." He attributed her refusal to have sex to her "feeling fat," an unsubtle body-shaming tactic. Asked during cross-examination about his initial denial that intercourse occurred, before DNA was detected on her tights, he piled on more insult with a shrug: "I guess it was not memorable."

More classic victim-blaming questions followed. Why,

the defense attorney pressed, didn't she flee? Overpowered, feeling helpless during the assault, she stopped fighting and froze. This response, known as tonic immobility or rape paralysis, is an adaptive strategy of shutting down physical responsiveness to ward off attackers. It is the most common response to rape, experienced—involuntarily—by roughly 70 percent of victims. The mind of the prey, lizards and mammals alike, freezes in a state of high alarm, to dissociate from the violence that seems inevitable. "I was like a trapped animal. There was nothing for me to do," she recalled.

The defense attorneys played up their mystification, asking: Why did the victim contact her assailant eleven days after the assault? Twenty-five percent of victims of acquaintance rape seek out contact with their perpetrator, sometimes electing sex, to deny the violation, to compartmentalize fear, and to restore a feeling of control. The posttraumatic response of appeasing the person who causes harm maps onto gender training for many women, who are socialized to be amenable, people pleasing, and conflict avoidant. I hoped the jurors would understand that the victim's contact with the perpetrator had to do with a history of abandoning herself and directing anger inward, based on her low expectations about how she should be treated in the world.

Why, the defense questioned, had the victim held on to the unwashed semen-stained tights she wore that night? "A trophy," the defense attorney insisted during my cross-examination. "Isn't that right?" He was comparing the garment to the blue dress that Monica Lewinsky, a wildly misunderstood scapegoat, wore and preserved following her encounter in the Oval Office with President Clinton. The victim in this case had tucked the tights in the back of a drawer. As her therapist, I knew it was a way to emotionally compartmentalize her associations to the tights, while preserving the evidence of what happened to her.

Rape does not happen on a continuum, but rape myths persist because any of us is prone to minimize rape allegations, to imagine gray areas and nuance where there are none, if the alternative is to grapple with the commingling of helplessness and badness among us. As the jurors were reminded, the defendant may be a respected talent *and* a rapist. He may not rape all women he befriends, he may be upstanding in some areas of his life, and he may even identify with the victim's feeling of helplessness. Nonetheless, he twisted the story of what happened to his own benefit, claiming victimhood and referring to himself as the "underdog." He exploited modern versions of masculinity, casting himself as a broken, confused man, "a flawed human being." He was scared, he told the jury, showcasing his vulnerability while projecting his badness onto others: "I don't know why women, or anyone, would lie." His case hinged on the culture's penchant to sympathize with men who claim they want to evolve and to blame and bully women who dare to call them out.

The jury found him liable on all counts and awarded the rape survivor punitive damages. Rape, the jury made clear, is immoral, malicious, and causes lasting pain and suffering. And rape myths are no longer persuasive. Instead, they reveal an outdated refusal to imagine that no really does mean no. Blaming victims, casting shade, body shaming, and relying on female silence is not a good gamble. Indeed, there are no safe victims.

In my sessions with the victim years before, I had tried to offer therapeutic solace: "The worst has already happened." With this harrowing trial and the validation of the court behind her, she's helped pave the way for other survivors who need this sentiment to be true.

Walking out of the courthouse, elated by the guilty verdict, I passed the rapist with his shoulders hunched, audibly crying, embracing his adult children. I thought about how this whole trial could have been avoided. What happened to him long ago that led him to disown his vulnerability and to deposit it into the women he raped? Even after he committed rape, why couldn't he reckon with the source of his pain, acknowledge the hurt he caused, grapple with his moral failing, and make amends? Instead, without remorse, he mounted a multimillion-dollar defense, hiding behind rape myths and legalese, while subjecting the victim to intense scrutiny and objectification in the courtroom.

"It seems wrong, but I feel sad for him," I said to a journalist friend as we passed through the rotunda, beyond the metal detector. I perceived a man stripped of the emotional defenses he'd spent a lifetime building.

"You're human. Empathy is not a crime. We need more of it, not less," my friend offered. I found comfort in the emotional clarity of the Mennonite women who recognized that male aggression is fostered in toxic environments. They fled with their young children, filled with hope that their sons' humanity, nurtured empathically, could reverse a legacy of rape. ■

**Linda Michaels**
lindamichaels@psian.org

# When Talkspace Sued PsiAN and Me

After an ad aired widely featuring Michael Phelps talking about having felt suicidal and then endorsing "therapy for all," the first compliment arrived. The ad, with Michael first lying on the bottom of an empty pool that's windblown with dead leaves and then (bizarrely) sitting in an overstuffed armchair in the middle of the barren pool, was polished, professional. With its broad, sweeping message and high production value, it felt like a public service announcement for the betterment of society. A colleague sent an email to a professional listserv, stating, "Kudos to PsiAN and their efforts at bringing the importance of talk therapy to public awareness."

The congratulations turned into confusion; the fantasy—not least of which included where the Psychotherapy Action Network (PsiAN) might have gotten the funding or connections required to pull off such an ad—dissolved immediately. Others quickly chimed in to say this was a paid promotional appearance of the Olympian by Talkspace. Talkspace was an online company that sold primarily text messaging services to consumers as a means to communicate with licensed therapists. They also sold phone and video packages at higher prices and claimed to be the future of therapy. The compliment seemed surprising since, far from endorsing the kinds of therapy of depth, insight, and relationship that are central to PsiAN's mission, Talkspace predominantly sold text services that seemed to simulate therapy. Adding to the surprise was the fact that PsiAN had been in existence for only a little over a year. Yes, we had grown rapidly. Yes, we had ambitious goals to change the public's narrative about therapy. But we were far from being able to engage someone like Phelps on national TV.

Alarmed by the appeal of this ad and its presumptive definition of therapy, the two other PsiAN co-founders, Nancy Burke and Janice Muhr, and I started to research Talkspace[1]. This was May 2018, well before the pandemic and before many of us had ever contemplated seeing a patient on Zoom.

In that phenomenon where once you see something new, then you see it all around you, I learned that a therapist who sublet an office in our suite had worked for Talkspace. She said she did so for several months right after she got licensed, was at home with a new baby, and didn't yet have a job. She thought it sounded like it was a good idea given her circumstances; she said, however, that it was awful. There were scripts she had to learn and use—not so much for how to respond to the customer's presenting issues or clinical concerns but for sales purposes, i.e., say X at the beginning with a new client, say Y if the customer wants to stop using Talkspace, say Z to try to upgrade the customer to more lucrative phone or video sessions. It was clear that therapists were trained into dual relationships, at once therapists to their clients and salespeople for

1 We benefited from the research and writings of Todd Essig, who had taken up the Talkspace issue several years prior in a series of articles for *Forbes* outlining the misleading claims and potential harms inherent in Talkspace's business model and terms of service. More fuel was added to the fire when we saw the APA's *Monitor on Psychology* featuring an ad from Talkspace, inviting psychologists to come "join the future of therapy."

Talkspace. She said that the therapist's "trainers," who were not clinicians, read the transcripts of the text messages exchanged between the customer and the therapist. Their interest was in ensuring that therapists were following the scripts and maximizing every opportunity to retain a customer and/or upsell them; of course, this means there was no real confidentiality for customers. These revenues certainly weren't going to this therapist; for six months of work at Talkspace, she made $600.

On July 9, 2018, we channeled our alarm and outrage into a letter we sent to the advertising managers at the American Psychological Association (APA) and Michael Phelps. We ginned up our courage and sent the letter to the president and CEO of the APA and the CFO/COO of the APA, as well as to the APA listserv of analytic psychotherapists (division 39). Curiously, within twenty-four hours we received an email from Oren Frank, the CEO of Talkspace. Oren invited us to meet with him and Talkspace's chief medical officer and VP of research and development. A day later—before we had time to contemplate a response to Oren and before we understood how he got ahold of our letter—Talkspace sent us a cease-and-desist letter. They demanded an "immediate retraction" of our letter and were kind enough to suggest an apology we might offer as well! The cease-and-desist letter arrived on Friday, July 13, at 4:15 p.m. and said, "If Talkspace does not receive a copy of a full retraction of all false statements by the end of business July 15, 2018, it will begin preparations of civil legal proceeding on all counts."

Alarm and outrage surged again. This scare tactic was having its intended effect, and it took every bit of those panic-reducing approaches I share with my patients in times of high anxiety to calm myself. We reached out to the lawyers who had worked with us pro bono to set up PsiAN's nonprofit status. They agreed that Talkspace was overstepping and trying to intimidate us and silence our free speech. In an incredible effort that I deeply respect and am profoundly grateful for, they wrote a twelve-page comprehensive and muscular letter to Talkspace, defending PsiAN's arguments, our right to free speech, and our decision to "neither retract [our] publication nor apologize for [its] content." We did not hear back from Talkspace. Our days of anxiety and fear, followed by our sleepless nights, wound down.

We also felt shimmers of victory when the APA wrote us on July 23, stating that "after thoughtful deliberation, a decision was made to cancel Talkspace advertising and exhibit space going forward in APA publications and at the APA Convention." This left only a few days of celebration, because at the APA annual convention the following month, attendees were given name badges with a lanyard branded by BetterHelp, another online platform similar to Talkspace! Although this felt like a slap in the face of every psychologist, Janice, Nancy, and I felt that the official change in APA policy was meaningful and that we could recover from the sting of sticking our necks out there.

In March 2019, we celebrated with everyone else when the Wit v. United Behavioral Health (UBH) class-action lawsuit ended with a landmark victory for the people. UBH was found to have put its own financial interests above patient welfare. UBH created its own guidelines to determine whether it would cover treatment. Not only did these internal guidelines fail to meet generally accepted standards of care, but they were heavily influenced and ultimately controlled by UBH's finance department—not its clinical team. When coverage was granted, it was mainly for controlling acute symptoms or crises, while coverage for more chronic or underlying issues was denied. The plaintiffs included representation of individuals who had died as a result of UBH's failure to pay for their care.

Just a few months later, I was pummeled by disbelief when UBH and Talkspace announced they were entering into a partnership. These two companies were at the top of my list of those degrading and corrupting mental healthcare, and to learn that they were collaborating scared me. At PsiAN we dusted off our letter to the APA and wrote anew to the APA president. That very same day (did we have a mole on the PsiAN listserv? Did APA?), we received a cease-and-desist from Talkspace's lawyer; it had taken just a few hours for the consequences of speaking truth to power to hit us. We reached out to our lawyers again and met to discuss how they would respond. They said we had some time to formulate a response, and they would work on that. However, just a few weeks later, our lawyers informed us that Talkspace had filed a lawsuit in federal court in Washington, DC, against PsiAN and the cofounders, for defamation and libel, asking for $40 million in damages.

A few days after that, our lawyers resigned.

In a manic defense against the fear and desperation of being sued by a huge corporation while PsiAN had about $5,000 in the bank, we flung ourselves into a search for new lawyers. We were also told not to talk about this with anyone—one of the cruelest aspects of the legal system. Of course, the cofounders could pick up the phone to talk among ourselves—but no emailing or texting – and no communication with anyone else. I did talk with my partner and parents, but this enforced isolation at a point when I was engulfed by anxiety was a nearly intolerable punishment.

There was a deadline by which a legal response was required in the case, so we couldn't continue searching for a lawyer for long. In the deeply improbable search for an affordable attorney, I was surprised to receive a call from a lawyer in California. She expressed a lot of sympathy and anger; she was familiar with large corporations selling inferior products and then using these tactics to silence critics. She said she'd reach out to a colleague. We had so many calls like this provide some temporary relief but then lead nowhere, so I was surprised to get a call the next day from her colleague, Dori Hanswirth, in the New York office. Dori said she was outraged on our behalf and that she would discuss it with her firm and get back to us in a few days. The very next day, this compassionate, clear-minded, powerful lawyer said she got approval from her firm, Arnold & Porter, to represent us pro bono. After the initial shock of this tremendous offering wore off, I wept. I was overwhelmed by this decision of Dori and her firm—the validation from their investment in PsiAN, in our arguments against Talkspace and the threats it posed to patients, therapists, and the integrity of therapy itself. I was relieved and exhausted.

Dori and her team filed two motions for us in August and October 2019. Talkspace filed one motion in September 2019, and it was from their documents that we learned that Talkspace and APA had entered into a "strategic partnership consist[ing] of various Talkspace marketing materials in APA publications [...] and a contract wherein Talkspace agreed to sponsor the APA's 2018 annual convention." We were shocked to learn this. It was astonishing that APA would have partnered with Talkspace in these ways, even as Talkspace's business model was undermining the field. And we learned for the first time the full impact of our 2018 letter to the APA; indeed, Talkspace's CEO declared that PsiAN "successfully pressured the APA to withdraw from our sponsorship." That finally explained why we heard from Oren directly; perhaps he was the first one APA contacted when they received our 2018 letter.

As an example of the absurdity of Talkspace's lawsuit, they sued us in Washington, DC, because that's the only jurisdiction nationwide where we could not immediately say that this was a SLAPP suit, a frivolous lawsuit to silence criticism that clearly violates First Amendment rights to free speech. To rationalize its choice of the DC venue, Talkspace claimed that PsiAN owned property in DC. The truth? One of PsiAN's cofounders, Janice Muhr, cosigned for her daughter's rental apartment while she attended law school there.

The case was dismissed by the judge, Beryl Howell, who was otherwise very busy with the Mueller investigation, in January 2020. We held our breath for another six months, during which Talkspace could have refiled the lawsuit in the correct jurisdiction. We exhaled six months later and celebrated quietly. Although I was quoted in a *New York Times* exposé about Talkspace in August 2020, we haven't publicized our Talkspace experience widely. Not until a recent article that features our experience with Talkspace and this one did I feel sufficiently safe to revisit all this.

Since the lawsuit against us, Talkspace's fortunes have suffered significantly. Their two founders, their COO, and several CEOs have been removed and replaced. Talkspace went public in 2021, yet is itself being sued by investors who claim that Talkspace misrepresented its financials to them. From a high of $11 a share, Talkspace's stock is now worth about 80 cents. Talkspace's products continue to compromise users' privacy and confidentiality, as rated by an independent nonprofit.

In stark contrast, PsiAN continues to grow and expand its reach and impact. Our membership now stands at nearly 5,500 individuals and almost 90 organizations. We've published our first journal issue, a position paper on mental health apps and technology, and most recently, our first book, *Advancing Psychotherapy for the Next Generation: Humanizing Mental Health Policy and Practice*. We proudly joined the masthead of *ROOM*. I consulted on the John Oliver show *Last Week Tonight* for an episode focused on the mental health system, and we've recently written to the FTC about BetterHelp, a competitor of Talkspace, when the FTC was seeking to ban BetterHelp from sharing customer data internally and with Facebook and others for advertising purposes, especially after BetterHelp had promised repeatedly to keep such data private.

Bruised and battered and somewhat more sanguine about what it takes to advocate in the public sphere, we continue our work at PsiAN. I never want to face down another multimillion-dollar lawsuit or relive the terror of a corporate bully—my system couldn't handle the cortisol—but I am energized every day by our mission. The threats to psychoanalysis and depth therapy are too great, and the public's dire need for reliable information and therapy that works is too important. We cannot leave it to corporations to address these needs or fill these voids, and we must hold them to account. We still don't have anywhere near the amount of money needed to get Phelps swimming in our lane, but knowing that all the gloss and chlorine money can buy is still vulnerable to organized voices gives me hope. It takes a village to humanize healthcare. ■

# Investigations

## A Short Story

**Philip Brunetti**
philipbrunetti.com

The mayor called for an investigation into the amount of horseshit that's been accumulating on Central Park West as of late. 'It's a veritable dumping ground,' one disgusted resident said.

'It's a lot of shit,' the mayor was quoted as saying. 'I meant caca or crap. You know what I meant,' he added.

Anyway the mayor said they'd be starting a proper investigation. The right agency or investigative body would be called upon to proceed. In this case, the Department of Sanitation, but there were suggestions of a new agency potentially being formed. Code name: the Shit Squad.

An investigation into a neighborhood 'poet' may be imminent and possibly already underway. There is a middle-aged man who shows up regularly at neighborhood hotspots and sits and acts frigid and still. Sometimes he scribbles in a notebook. He appears to be living in some kind of inward space or trance-like state, but an investigation would, or at least could, uncover a more accurate assessment.

'We've never seen a poet in these parts,' a neighborhood resident said. 'We don't like it. The world may be dying—but this guy's no good.'

As a sidebar, a long-ago girlfriend of the alleged poet was questioned in Jacksonville, Florida. She stated that when they'd dated in New York decades earlier, she was the 'Femme Baudelaire of Brooklyn.' Unacknowledged in her time. 'He's in my footsteps,' she added.

Another Boeing 777 has disappeared without a trace into the vast recesses of the overlap between the Indian and Pacific Oceans. The missing airplane is the same make and model as Malaysia Airlines Flight 370, which disappeared en route to Beijing in March of 2014. An investigation into that prior plane disappearance bore no definitive fruit, and investigators are worried that the similar trajectory of the current missing flight may be doomed to the same void of information. They are, however, trying to stay optimistic. Eerily though, 228 people, including both passengers and crew—the exact number as the ill-fated Malaysian flight—are now missing and presumed dead.

An investigation into Florida is pending. It seems that some diabolical or horrible entity has that peninsular state by the proverbial throat. Florida's murder rate is one of the highest per capita in the nation and, therefore, the civilized world. There is more violent death in Florida than ever before, and an investigation has been necessitated by the grim facts on the ground. In addition to the state's outrageous record of both legal and illegal gun ownership, legal precedents such as "Stand Your Ground" have greatly increased the death rate.

'People just go out and stand on the corner with a weapon holstered or strapped to their backs. They stand there until someone comes around and enters their orbit. Usually, then, within moments a round or rounds are fired off.'

Stand your ground—kill or be killed. An orange blossom (the official state flower) by any other name...as sweet.

The expiration dates on Puffy Pop popcorn are being investigated for possible forgery or inaccuracy. Over the past several months, too many Puffy Pop foil hats haven't inflated fully, and many of the brown kernels within have not exploded open. 'The evidence is that these expiration dates are incorrect or the corn's just no good. There could also be a manufacturing error exacerbating this,' a spokesperson said.

The focus, however, will be on the stamped expiration dates themselves, as they're purplish, not the standard black, and are dubiously printed in Roman numerals.

An investigation into the president's shoe size is now underway. This is the first president in history whose shoe size has reportedly increased by three sizes while in office. At the outset of his presidency, the president wore (an average) size 10, and now, just three years later, he's been seen purchasing—or at least wearing—size 13. With one brand in particular, the size reading was 13.5. Some skeptics have wondered if this isn't just a case of very thick socks or doubled socks or poorly trimmed, clawlike toenails necessitating extra shoe space. Others have suspected real growth due to steroid usage as the president's jawline also seems altered and more muscular, which some point to as a telltale sign.

'Remember Barry Bonds,' one commentator put in. 'He had biceps cheeks. And his cleat size—not to mention his hat size—grew dramatically due to steroid use. Hell, his homerun 'size' grew largest of all (chuckle).'

The president's hat size hasn't been easily traceable, as the president eschews hats and also dislikes tape measures wrapped around his head and hair in particular. However, further investigations into these size increases will continue with or without the president's cooperation. Likely without it.

'Holy! Holy! Holy! Holy! Holy! Holy! Holy! Holy! Holy! Holy! Holy! Holy! Holy! Holy! Holy!' An investigation into the number of 'Hol[ies]' that appear toward the end of Allen Ginsberg's famous Beat poem 'Howl' is now underway. Sources say a draft initially submitted to City Lights, the poem's original (and only legal) publisher, may have actually contained only fourteen repetitions of the exclamation 'Holy!'—preceding the statement 'The World is Holy!'—rather than the published fifteen. Some Beat Generation scholars are tiptoeing around this finding, and some are simply saying it's a holy goof on City Lights' part.

Neither Allen Ginsberg nor City Lights' founding editor, poet, and publisher, Lawrence Ferlinghetti, are alive still to assist with the investigation. However, a manuscript page, supposedly written in Ginsberg's own hand, shows a slash through the second-to-last 'Holy!' causing some scholars to question the poet's numerically 'holy' intentions.

An investigation into 3-K and pre-K graduation rates has begun. The crux of the investigation is that both 3-K and pre-K students are graduating to the next grade level simply due to their getting older. 'We've got pre-K graduates that don't even know their circles from their squares. A 3-K graduate mistook blue for green. But because they reach the age of four or five, they're moved to the next grade. It's a sham—it inflates graduation rates—and it isn't right. Period.'

Investigations will be—and in some cases have already been—scrutinizing the testing data on these intellectually teetering tots. More tot-damning information is expected to be forthcoming.

A young child with chocolate on his fingers and mouth was questioned in the (dis)appearance of a torn-through box of chocolates found under the family kitchen table. The child is only five or six years old, and the box of chocolates contained 20–25 pieces. By the time the child was confronted, the chocolate high had become a raging headache. Strangely and coincidentally, as the child was being forced into his bedroom for a curative nap, he kept screaming that Ferlinghetti was alive and well and still writing at the age of one hundred.

The child's chocolate-inspired, near-overdose tirade also included a few quotes from 'A Coney Island of the Mind.' Chocolate was still being vigorously wiped off his mouth and hands with a warm wet towel. As he faded into sleep, an avuncular family member entered the child's room and began reading excerpts from Henry Miller's Black Spring, 'A Coney Island of the Mind' section (from which Ferlinghetti's poem takes its title). Miller remains dead, but an investigation is pending into Ferlinghetti's status and potential whereabouts.

The term 'active shooter' is being investigated for being potentially offensive to an active shooter. 'The shooter's rights are delimited, as this term is overly reductive to the totality of the human being holding the gun,' a terminology objector stated. 'This is a progressive's nightmare,' a stray commentator put in.

Different solutions to the biased terminology are being explored, and one suggestion being floated is to provide the active shooter with a questionnaire listing numerous synonymous terms such as 'flowing trigger-puller,' 'mobile weapon-wielder,' and the like. The shooter would then check off his top three choices. Being that there are now active shooters nearly every day, if not multiple times a day, useful data could be quickly obtained and an approved alternate term then utilized.

An investigation into whether this story is true or fiction is dependent on whether Ferlinghetti is still alive and still 100 years old. Once either of those facts has changed, then the story will no longer be true. However, even if those facts hold for the duration of Ferlinghetti's one hundredth to his one hundred and first year, the story remains fiction. And it's unlikely any investigation will alter that.

An investigation into the length of investigations is now forthcoming. It has been pointed out that in addition to more investigations than ever occurring these days, there has also been an uptick in the length of time spent on them. In the trackable past, few investigations lasted for multiple years. Now a multiple-year investigation is more or less the norm.

'And it doesn't seem to matter whether you're investigating popcorn or the dead. Everything's taking longer—at least everything of the investigative sort. Remember that horseshit investigation they used to talk about? Well, the shit's still there on CPW, and the Shit Squad is still investigating. Hell, I think they're still being formed. So when is any of this stuff going to be wrapped up?'

An investigation into when these investigations will wrap up is pending.

An investigation into the specific words that came out of the chocolate-filching-and-gobbling child's mouth has revealed that he said, 'Ferlinghetti's 100 and something and still writing!' If this statement meets full corroboration, then the true and false factors of this short fiction may be reevaluated as a result of said investigation. Please stand by.

An investigation into 'the depth of sadness' has begun. 'Even if this investigation has a bit of a pretentious bent, I think it's worth doing,' one of the data collectors said.

As a measuring tool, sadness has been broken down into a color grid of different shades of blue, gray, and black. Other borderline colors may also make up the utilized color map. 'I don't think the data on this will really uncover anything about the depth of sadness,' a neighborhood philosopher asserted. This same philosopher also stated that he isn't a philosopher but a local sufferer of sadness.

'I do have my heavier thoughts at times, but I don't think they add up to a "philosophy,"' he stated, using finger quotes for 'philosophy.' 'Anyhow, depth is depth and data are just data.'

When questioned about the phrase "the depth of sadness," proponents of this investigative survey were hesitant to expound on the exact meaning and said they were ultimately unsure of what such depth could conclusively mean.

'I guess what we're talking about here is mass depression or something worse even. Maybe we're trying to investigate our way out of some grand malaise. That'd be a neat trick. But really, all I can say, as far as the depth of sadness goes, is, who knows?'

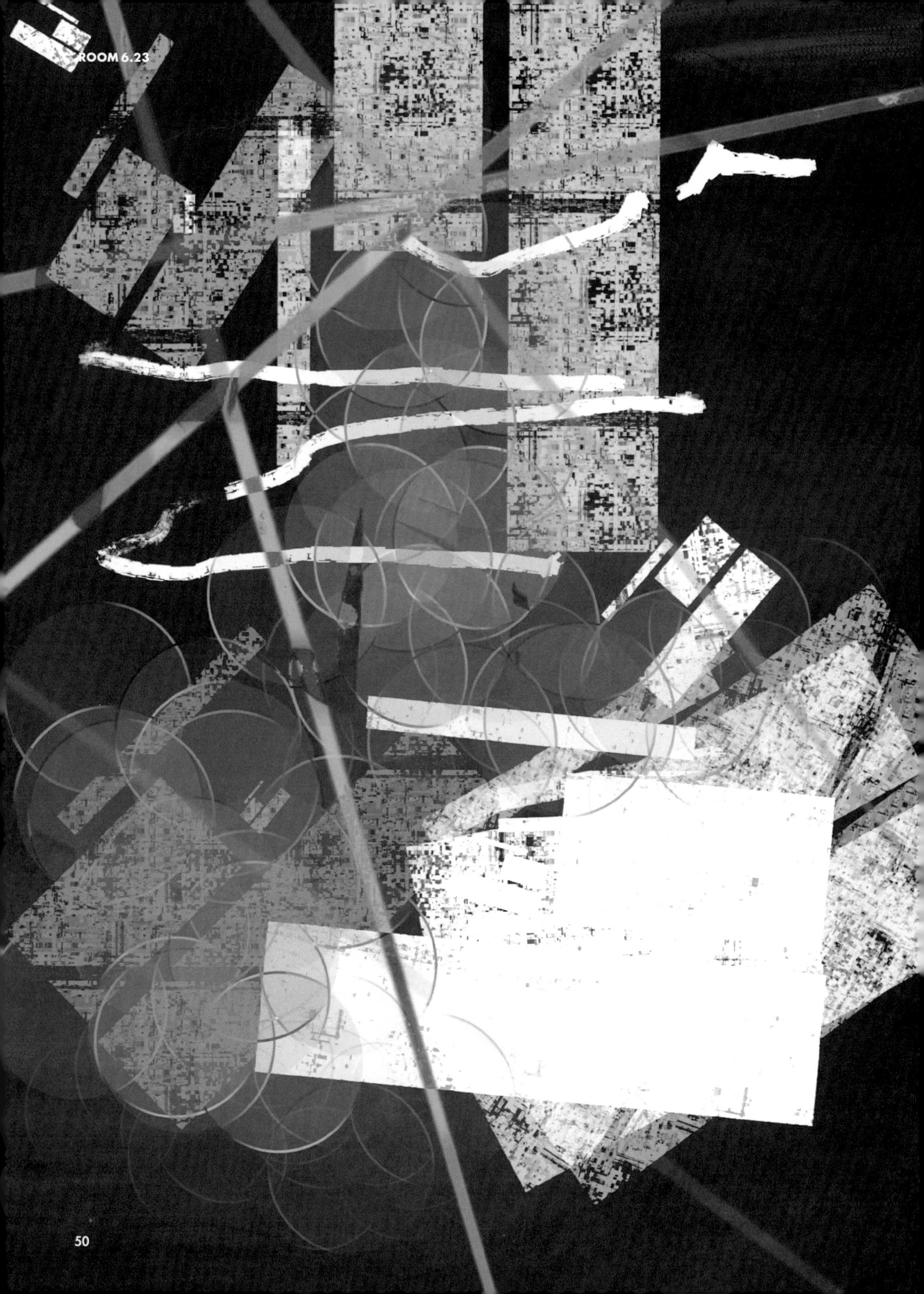

**Stephanie Niu**
niustephanie@gmail.com



# Phenomenology

is the kind of word that vanishes
from my mind as soon as I look it up.

I Google Michel Leiris. No faster way
to forget a man. I try to follow

*the tenuous thread of the sentence.*
Sentience must be a similarly delicate

string, airborne maple seed.
The first time I caught snow

on my tongue and tilted my head back
to watch white whirl from the dark

I thought, whose globe am I in?
The flight only visible in street lamps' lobes

of light. Any flake I touched was gone.
Any flake the world touched was gone,

whirl stilled, seconds pooled
to leave nothing but the sound

*gone*, and the word. My mind left
with only a *gallery of words*.

---

The italicized text quotes Gaston Bachelard's introduction to "Poetics of Space," p.11-12. The introduction references J.B. Pontalis' "Michel Leiris ou la psychanalyse interminable," which describes Leiris as a "lonely prospector in the galleries of words."

**Chaim Rochester**
chaim.rochester@gmail.com



# Carol

I met Carol when I was in my early twenties. She was sweet and funny, with a gravelly Jersey accent and a streetwise tomboy persona. I don't know how she ended up homeless and turning tricks on the streets of Sin City, but we crossed paths in the circle of transient addicts I was running with at the time and took to each other immediately—the fast bond of street siblings that often occurs between the desperate and the damned.

She was rough and crude but with a dream still left inside her. She got excited about simple things; a few extra bucks from a generous client or a nice outfit from the discard container out behind the Savers thrift store and her face would light up with a smile and a contented laugh. Most people I met in that world were like that: frayed and weary but vital. Buoyed by a particular kind of survivor's optimism. This tenacity was an essential tool for survival. For the sick, the mad, the shadow dwellers — all those who had slipped through the cracks while no one was looking, who had gone untended or unseen while the neglectful mechanics of the world were playing themselves out in homes and schools and institutions all across the many lands that reared us—hope was sometimes a dangerous thing, but its absence was fatal.

I had a shabby apartment in a complex a few blocks off the Strip, paid for by way of a succession of manipulative, guilt-soaked phone calls to my mother, who had not yet become able to ignore my narcotic insanity. At some point Carol and I struck an arrangement: I'd spend my days out hustling and scavenging, and she would be off turning tricks for her Johns, and at the end of the day we'd meet at my place to pool our take and score some dope. She would shower while I made us a beggar's meal, and we'd get high, eat, and talk awhile before nodding off next to each other on the cheap full-size mattress included in my weekly rent.

We were never physical. It was a relationship of emotional proximity and guarded vulnerability that allowed us to share in a measure of solace, each clinging to the ballast of momentary companionship as we struggled to survive the madness of our disparate afflictions. She was a child of abuse and violence and I one of self-loathing and faithless defiance. We were, truly, a gift to each other in that time and space. Each of us was the only one who really saw the other, and in that we were afforded a reminder of our humanity amid the monochrome pallor that hung heavy as a shroud all around us.

I would often wake in the night to hear her grappling with the carnivorous demons of her dreams. She would jolt and thrash, protesting in a low moan and muttering echoes out of her past.

"No, no, Mama, stop it!"

"I'm sorry. I didn't mean to be bad. I won't do it anymore!"

I would lie there, horrified and helpless, holding the fragility of these unseen traumas like a sparrow's bones. I dared not put an arm around her, but my every instinct was crying out to take action, to help, to console—to fix. And there were my own fear and emptiness to contend with. I was also weak, longing for relief and understanding. In the absence of a means of relief, my divergent sadness suggested physical comfort, as if I could open my arms and absorb her pain in some way, to show us both that we were going to be okay. As if I could protect her and we could both be safe and free from the tyranny of our fermenting grief.

These thoughts came and went quickly, and they troubled me. I pushed them away, recoiling from the impulse and knowing that it wasn't the right answer, that you can't fight fire with electricity, but still feeling that I should do something. As I lay there in a paralytic state of sympathetic uncertainty, I found the space to contemplate the greater scope of the moment. She was caught in the psychic damage of her experience, and I was drowning in a deluge of emptiness. And there we were: Lost. Human. Together. How could I say that she needed to be saved? Or that my instinct to comfort was to be rejected as necessarily wrong? What value judgments was I placing on things beyond my control or understanding, and why did I feel compelled to rush to action? Here were two fragile, wounded people trapped in our shadows and living outside the frame of normal society in a fugue of fear, pain, and isolation, and we knew each other. Did that knowing require an attendant solution? I was her witness and her safety, and she, mine. Perhaps silent recognition was all we had been called there to provide. For a brief time, we found something between us that was greater than the sum of our fears. In our own peculiar way, we were family, lending to each other's survival.

In the years following, I have thought of her often, wondering if she made it out and found a life she could live with, as so many I knew during those years did not. As I think of Carol and mourn the anniversaries of the passing of other companions who I know did not survive their war against the crushing indifference of the modern world, I have also thought of my own shift in that experience, of traversing the spaces between the purgatory of fearful isolation, the conflict of polluted empathy, and the acceptance of powerless solidarity. When I step outside my home and see all those who are still routinely swept to the margins, I cannot make sense of the fact that I am here. Casting back to that shared bare mattress in the dark of night, I see it now from a new perspective. Sometimes the work is to look inward. Sometimes the work is to join. Sometimes the work is to witness. All these require us to continuously develop our capacities to listen, to learn, and to concern ourselves, to make ourselves available—in the right way at the right time—to those who might be carrying a weight we cannot feel, cannot fix, and can never truly comprehend. ■

**Anaís Martinez Jimenez**
aimj@princeton.edu



# Carmela

## A Short Story

**"Face presentation. Deep mentum transverse," said the doctor. The baby's chin was facing the birth canal. There was no way to keep pushing for a natural birth. Carmela was grateful she had planned for this. At least, in her mind she had.**

No one dared mention the word "cesarean" at Perla's baby shower. Carmela was sitting at the round table with the other women of the ladies' committee. Perla was a celebrated woman in their small city, one of six daughters, a destined entrant into the sacred cult of maternity to which some already belonged and all others aspired. With Perla's "rite of passage" on the horizon, the women pontificated about orgasmic births and patterned breathing exercises. They spoke as if a cesarean weren't an option at all. Besides Perla, Carmela was the only other pregnant woman there. She looked at Perla across the table and tried to tap her with her stare—it worked. It usually did. It was one of those things she couldn't explain, but Carmela was certain that if she stared at someone long and hard enough, she would eventually coax at least a short glance in return.

Perla met her gaze—she was thinking about it too. The other women at the table had forgotten or had no idea what it was like to fear for one's life in those dark private moments of the night—the few seconds when no one was listening and no one could catch you in the thought-act—*What if this creature kills me on its way out?*

Carmela found it all so absurd, the world's perverted obsession with natural birth. Of all things, why was this the singular process that required a woman to proceed without synthetic intervention? She thought of ripping wax, digging girdles, hot combs. But this drug, which allowed for the preservation of a birthing woman's organs and sanity, which could create some space between the joy and pain, the soul and the body—why not?

Perla yielded first, broke the eye contact. It was a clear message. Whatever her thoughts were about the birthing question, she was not committing them to conversation. Carmela understood. Nevertheless, she had thought deeply about the possibility of a cesarian and had decided that she found it even more natural than the other barbaric mess.

...

Labor was progressing. The nurses said they couldn't wait any longer. They began wheeling Carmela to the operating room they had prepared. Carmela reveled in an odd feeling of relief and determination. She was able to take her spirit, commend it into the body of her little baby, and all would be well. Her flesh could be discarded if need be.

The anesthesiologist came into the room with the spinal tap. They sat her up to insert the tube. Everyone waited for a few minutes.

"Can you feel that?" asked the doctor, scalpel in hand.

"Yes!" shrieked Carmela.

"Breathe, sweetie. Breathe."

He turned to the nurse. "It's been long enough; the catheter might have disconnected. It could be the scoliosis. Try again."

Twenty minutes passed. The doctor had been testing Carmela with small cuts. She screamed in agony each time. She was feeling everything, and she could especially feel every slit, stealing that initial resolve. Cut by cut, her screams grew louder and louder, her worry deeper and deeper. This was not as simple as death. This was not a clean sacrifice. She kept herself from pushing for what felt like hours until, with a final scream, her body took over.

"I'm sorry. This is going to hurt, but we have to go now, we have to go, we have to go," said the doctor.

She could hear all the voices in the room at once: loud, fast, crashing against each other. And then, above it, the most bloodcurdling scream. It went on and on and on. Years later, it hadn't stopped. Like a beast, it roared, yelling, "No! Please no!" Carmela's ears were overcome by a high-pitched ringing, and she could feel her body turned inside out—her arms tied to the sides of the bed, her head rolled back in anguish. She saw herself from above—stretched on that table, mouth gaping—yet somehow invisible, inaudible, completely forgotten.

Black...scream...black...scream...black.

2.

If Carmela didn't take the girl to get a haircut that Friday morning, it would never happen. The girl miraculously had the day off from school—some teacher's retreat, some generic excuse. She would use the time, when the other kids were out of the house, to finally go get the fringe cut out of the little girl's eyes.

There was not much there to begin with. The girl hadn't completely outgrown her infantile wisps. Clips would slide right off, and hair products seemed like cement against her meadow of a head. She would tell the hairdresser to cut it all off. She'd ask for something short and practical.

Theresa, the housekeeper, had already called her three times about the things they were missing from the cleaning cabinet.

"I can't be ready unless I have Fabuloso and rubber gloves," said Theresa.

Carmela really needed the place to be ready for the guests this time. She had to delay her first event by an hour and a half because she had forgotten to move the Christmas boxes out of the shed and the caterers needed the space for drinks and ice. She and Theresa had pulled out the boxes, and Carmela, allowing herself no sentimental attachments, threw out almost everything—old stockings, handmade ornaments, tangled tinsel. The little girl had been sitting on the floor while they cleaned, and she managed to find the dry carcass of a small dead cockroach behind one of the boxes. Carmela stared in horror as the guileless toddler picked up the insect and put it right in her mouth. "No!" she yelled, and frantically slapped the girl's lips. But she couldn't bring herself to stick in her fingers and pull the thing out.

Carmela was thrilled with her new business. The children spent most of their time out front anyway. Those enormous backyards were no longer practical. The smaller front yard suited them all better. Besides, the only one who spent any time outside anyway was the little girl. She would spend hours out front, chasing the dog and picking up stunned birds. Most of all, she loved to stand on her head.

"Mamá, look, look, look! Look, look, look, look!"

She would take a few steps back, point one little foot, and throw herself forward and down. Carmela would see her frantically stretch her legs toward the sky before tipping over and landing on the grass with a thump. She would do it again and again with an almost compulsive determination, all the time begging her to witness the awkward attempts.

Turning the backyard into a rental party venue was the best idea Carmela ever had. She would manage the business from home, offer Theresa as a waitress for an extra charge, and eventually buy those used slides from the restaurant that was closing near the highway. This was their third fully rented weekend. Friday, Saturday, and Sunday all booked. Carmela knew that if she wanted the three days to run successfully, she had to make sure she was prepared from the get-go.

Parking was a nightmare. They could say all they wanted that this city was the "San Francisco of Mexico." But at least they built the houses in San Francisco straight up. These homes were almost perpendicular to the slope of the hills. Every one of the unfashionable old houses had water damage and cracked walls. And it wasn't easy to parallel-park while on a forty-five-degree incline.

They were asked to sit down as soon as they arrived at the hair salon. It was one of those cheap places. The kind you visit once and never again lest they confuse you for a regular. Once and never again. There were so many cheap salons in the city. You could go to a different one every day of the year if you wanted to.

The little girl was overly excited. Carmela could see her staring at the posters of big-breasted women with neon hair hanging on the walls of the salon. The little girl was probably wondering where in the world people looked like that. Carmela wondered the same thing.

They were finally next. Carmela was already mapping her exit route in her mind: get Fabuloso, pick up the tablecloths from the dry cleaners, bring them home. Everything was within a five-minute drive. It wasn't going to take long.

Carmela started feeling dizzy—hair-dye fumes. She had become so sensitive to smells, tastes, sounds. It was going to be another thirty minutes, at least, before they sat the girl down. Theresa was calling again. Carmela went up to the hairdresser.

"Look, I just want the girl's hair to be as manageable as possible. Cut it short and straight across."

"Yes, okay, we'll be right with you," said the woman.

"No, look, I have to run some errands really quickly. It won't take more than twenty minutes. Let me leave her here with you. I'll just go drop off a few things, and I'll pick her up when you're done. I'll probably be back before you even start."

"Umm, okay, sure! But we close early today, so please don't be late."

"Oh, no! It will take fifteen minutes at most."

The woman who had rented the place that day was Perla's older sister, Maricarmen. She had a five-year-old and a three-year-old and she was throwing her older son a *101 Dalmatians*–themed party. The entire space was covered in black-and-white dots, and Maricarmen even paid a local pound to bring puppies for the children to play with. It wasn't the first time Carmela saw a mother go overboard for the sake of their child's initiation into the group. It had always been that way, every mother trying to one-up the last kid's party.

Maricarmen was a mess. She was drunk by the time the party began and had forgotten a handful of the party essentials: napkins, candles, a cake knife. Furthermore, the helium tank they usually used for the balloons, which was included in the rental cost, had run out of gas in the middle of decorating. But even while inebriated, Maricarmen was one of Carmela's most important clients. Her business ran on word of mouth, and she knew that Maricarmen and her sister were at the very center of the ladies' network.

Despite the drawbacks, the party was running successfully. Carmela gathered all the children to sing "Happy Birthday" and handed Maricarmen the cake knife. It was when Maricarmen took her son's hand to help him with the cake, right at the moment of the first cut, that Carmela remembered.

She sprinted to her car and started driving to the hair salon. The rush-hour traffic was always at its worst on Fridays. She sat anxiously, completely surrounded, and honked when the light turned green. She did not make it through the intersection before the light turned red again. She began to blink with its blinking and felt a thorn growing in her throat, her eyes burning with frustration. As she approached the steep hill where her daughter was waiting, the car began to slow down. She came to a stop at the side of the road and saw a second red light blinking on the dashboard.

She got out. There was no time to wait. She turned toward the hill and started toward her baby. She was half jogging at first—a bit desperate. But the incline began to weigh on her. She lengthened her stride as much as she could, but she could feel her thighs tightening, ripping. Her body was heavy, and her breathing disturbed by a clawing in her neck. She could not see in front of her—her eyes filled with sweat and salt. She was dragging her feet on the pavement, tripping on them. She felt a fever rising, but she continued so as not to lose her direction. The hill, the sun, the earth all pulling at her back. She walked and walked—the soles of her feet bloody, knees skinned, lips cracked. For scalding days, she walked a punishing passion, falling once, falling twice, falling three times.

She arrived at the place as the sun was setting. Her daughter was sitting on the curb, her hair half its original length. The hairdresser was talking to a police officer. Carmela apologized profusely, lied about having an emergency, and promised never to do it again. The man let her off with a scolding. She gave the hairdresser a large tip.

Carmela took her daughter's hand, and they started toward the car. The little girl was entirely silent. One block, two blocks...Carmela fell at her feet and sobbed thick, heavy tears on her baby's dress.

"Forgive me, my sweet girl...Please forgive me. I am sorry...I am sorry...I am so, so sorry." ■

*BOLTON LANDING*
*2021*
*48"x32"*
*oil/board*

## Mia Muratori

miamuratori.com



For me, artmaking is the documentation of what I see and seek to understand. Watching, synthesizing, recording, I lay it all down with paint, no words, just light, color, shape and space.

*ACTUALIZATION*
*2019*
*42"x30"*
*oil/canvas*

*PAUSE*
*2018*
*24"x18"*
*oil/canvas*

*THOUGHTS FLY UP*
*2018*
*36"x32"*
*oil/canvas*

**Libby Bachhuber**
lb@libbybachhuber.com



# What We Left Behind

My mind keeps returning to an image of myself sitting in my chair at the office—my therapist chair—in March 2023. Only the dim winter sun and the murmur of passing cars filtered in through the window on my left. Inside, the air purifier hummed. The couch across from me had been left empty when my patient stood to leave a few minutes before. I had closed the door behind her, then moved to my desk to retrieve my phone. Anticipating an unscheduled hour, I'd returned to my chair and lit up the screen, searching without thinking.

There's something faintly shameful and off-kilter about this memory, though it's also banal. Recalling it, I feel the emptiness of the room, the quiet after the vivacity of my previous patient. A moment before, we had been intent on her concerns about the future: her conflicting desires, her sense of powerlessness in the face of larger economic and political forces, her self-doubt, her hopes. The pandemic had upended her life in ways that she'd mostly welcomed, even as the virus scared her. She'd begun to question the premises of her life more deeply than ever before and to feel profound uncertainty about her next phase. Our hour together had been rich and full, if somewhat difficult. And then she was gone.

Years ago, I would have turned to my notebook to scribble a few phrases from the session. But in this memory, I turned to the phone instead, and the separation from her was handled through diversion instead of reflection. It had become a habit. On that afternoon, though, sitting in my chair, I became aware of a feeling of dissonance as I scrolled, and I pulled my attention away from the screen, back into myself. I experienced a sense of loneliness and the vague wish for human contact that had been pushing my search.

That's where the shame came in: shame about my need for contact and the way I was seeking it, shame that I had abandoned my patient and my work so quickly and impulsively. Judgments were surfacing about what I'm allowed to feel and do as a therapist—in my role, my chair. Yet it felt like I was contacting something important, something that hadn't always been there, about the ways that my own needs had come to be sidelined chronically. Sometimes those needs were stirred at the end of my time with patients. Now I could sense my anger too, and helplessness about the predicament of my isolation. But surely others are also feeling these things, alone in their therapy chairs. How did we get here, and why don't we talk about it?

That March afternoon echoes with earlier memories. Precisely three years before, in that same chair, I was working through what turned out to be the final week of in-person sessions; questions about the "novel coronavirus" were beginning to haunt my time with people. As I look back now, my images of those days—sitting with patients in my eleventh-floor office in downtown Chicago—are shadowed by my knowledge of what we were about to lose.

Over the course of those tense days in March 2020, questions turned to certainty: all plans needed to change. The next work week found me at home, as I began listening to patients through earbuds, huddled in the spare room, trying to ignore the sound of my three-year-old running up and down the hallway just outside the door. New worries entered the sessions, as patients struggled with uncertainty about their safety, their jobs, and their social responsibility in this time of collective crisis. I steadied myself with the task of re-creating our holding space, as if trying to listen intently on a lifeboat. And the container did seem to hold, miraculously, for them and for me, in session after session. But then a patient would share some disturbing piece of pandemic news, and my panic would rise as I remembered that I, too, was adrift on these stormy seas. I would fight the impulse to end the session and research this new information, to keep myself and my loved ones safe.

My phone was a lifeline. It kept the work going during a time when therapeutic relationships felt more crucial than ever. It connected me to family, friends, and mentors—we ran things by one another, reassuring and restabilizing again and again. And, of course, the phone and the internet brought me information. I remember watching, in those early weeks, a video of a physician in the COVID ward at a hospital somewhere in New York—Manhattan, I think. He acknowledged the weeks of overwhelm: patients on gurneys in hallways, unable to breathe; patients dying and being wheeled out to make room for more—all in an atmosphere of uncertainty about how this virus was transmitted and whether he would contract it and bring it home to his family. Ultimately, though, his video was a message of hope, based on a growing sense that, in his ward, their safety protocols were working; they were learning how to protect themselves. I held on to his words in the weeks that followed, as they intimated that this chaos might somehow be organized into a path forward. We wouldn't always have to live this way.

My rush to safety, in March 2020, meant retreating from face-to-face contact—bodies in a room. I was extremely lucky to be able to protect myself that way, and yet, when I think of it now, there's a pulse of feeling, like a buried sob.

I remember the life I left behind, where most of my human contact was in person. I hurried to and from meetings, greeted my friend and suitemate between sessions, tensed with faint nervousness when approaching a psychoanalytic lecture space, then softened when I saw familiar faces. Hour after hour, patients would visit my office, with me hosting them, in a way, implicitly welcoming them. When I think of it now, I understand the buried sob is about sudden absence, about people disappearing behind closed doors. It reminds me of the abandonment some clients felt when I announced we would begin meeting by phone.

I return to the image of being alone in my therapy chair—in March 2023. My next session was in an hour, with a longtime patient calling from his parents' home far outside the city, where he had moved at the beginning of the pandemic. It was my last session of the day. I decided to pack up and head home to take his phone call from there. I would do my own therapy appointment from home, too, so that I could get to my child's school just as it let out.

These phone sessions still feel complicated, though they've changed from those tumultuous early days. Now there can be something delicious about being home to do what used to require more separation from my life there. Like I'm stealing something back for myself. And yet there's an odd feeling about the whole thing, a split I feel during those calls. Part of me is focused intently on my patient, and another is rooted in my surroundings, my private space. My gaze may wander to the dusty corner of the shelf, the spine of the book I never got around to finishing, bright new maple leaves quivering beyond the window. With video sessions, too, and online meetings and lectures, the juxtaposition permeates the experience and strains my attention. We are together, sometimes in extraordinarily meaningful ways, and yet we are not together at all. The distance is rarely named.

Talking with colleagues, I hear us negotiating these splits—and adjusting the therapeutic frame—according to our own circumstances and leanings. In our decisions about meeting virtually, we consider the needs of our patients or meeting attendees but also our own concerns about health, finances, stressful commutes, domestic obligations, carbon footprints, etc. And then there are less-tangible pulls. At an in-person lecture, for example, we must face social differences, with their hierarchies and exclusions, an effort that demands more of us depending on our position in the community. When I attend the lecture from home, I can turn off my camera and sit in my socks. Something in me can relax. Maybe, for many who were able to spend more time at home during the pandemic, when we felt relatively safe there, certain neglected longings were stirred. The possibility of downplaying our human needs—ever present in our work—only increased under the countless pressures of these turbulent years. In certain situations, we may stay home as a way of rebalancing or even acting out our resentment. And the screen has come to seem good enough.

Truth be told, I was drawn out of my complacency after that first pandemic year by certain patients who kept wondering about meeting in person. I had been looking forward to finding an office closer to home, but after the first wave of vaccinations and the opening of the long-awaited Chicago summer, something in me seemed reluctant to "return to work" fully. Yet these patients seemed to know what they needed. Indeed, once I secured a suite, and we began sitting together again, I recognized what we had been missing. Even when we wore masks in those early months, our felt sense of one another deepened, and it opened more room for both conflict and silence. I remembered that I do this work, in part, to spend time with people in particular ways. There's something about the dance between two attentive mammals in a room.

Still, the dilemmas continue. Many of us are living with the echoes of unmourned losses and a flight to technology that began three years ago. We are left with forms of insularity and of distance communication that are partly chosen and partly habits we developed to cope. When we find ourselves in a dilemma about meeting or canceling, for example, we may opt for a virtual session without acknowledging the meanings and impacts of that choice. As a field, we seem to be neglecting these experiences, occluding them from our analytic view. And it may be difficult for that conversation to emerge spontaneously when Zoom is the main space for contacting acquaintances. We don't mingle much anymore.

There are needs that seem downplayed in all this, including the need to engage in embodied ways with people and concerns outside our immediate circle. For my part, I miss in-person psychoanalytic spaces, even as I appreciate what has been born from the gaps. I worry we are forgetting the significance of certain ways of being together that, as a community, we have re-created with one another year after year, decade after decade. Who would have thought, before the pandemic, that we could forget such a thing? Perhaps a form of dissociation is at work, protecting us from the sense of threat that forced our adaptations.

I wonder what might come of remembering and then opening to our feelings about what we have lost. We might have to face responses we feel we're not supposed to have and tensions that arise from our shifts in priorities and circumstances. We may come to recognize our longings for connection, our reluctance to connect, and the structural issues in our organizations that shape who connects with whom. But we might also be able to imagine new ways of working with all this, both in session and in collaboration with one another. First, though, we need to look back to what we left behind. ■

**Diane Raptosh**
draptosh@gmail.com



# The Score

When I become dust, I want to *Diane*
to be human for *Do not repeat where*
*we were.* I want it to shorthand how-to's.
How to upend: first, we re-nature. I want it
to plug for the land while sizing up griefs
of the day. To show how to stand for the self
while penciling notes on the trim of the world:
*Why it's queer to feel cared for: It's a fact about*
*life in America.* I would like my own action
verb to bank and clearwing. I want to id
and lever a din that heaps insistence on us
in the spore of its origin story. To have sung
as a sample person sheltering Earth. For you
to have oared these lines by the strobe of Venus.

# *Psychoanalysis Under Occupation: Practicing Resistance in Palestine*

By Lara Sheehi and Stephen Sheehi

Even a reader who agrees with the views implied in the title of *Psychoanalysis Under Occupation: Practicing Resistance* in Palestine may find this, as I did, to be an astonishing and revelatory book. The authors, Lara and Stephen Sheehi, a psychoanalyst and a humanities professor, respectively, of Arab Lebanese descent, introduce us to Palestinian patients and clinicians in order to bring their English-speaking readers into the lives and minds of Palestinians living under Israeli occupation. The two foci of the book are: the Occupation seen through the lens of psychoanalysis, and psychoanalysis under the conditions of the Occupation.

Their first focus, the Occupation, is to acquaint us with Palestinian patients and clinicians to make us feel the violence and humiliation that they are daily subjected to under Occupation by what the authors always term the "settler-colonial" power, that is, Israel.[1] Let us begin by considering the case of Amjad. A father of three, in his early thirties, Amjad presents for therapy due to a sensation of a lump or a ball in his throat whenever he becomes nervous. He is treated by a Palestinian therapist, who is supervised by an Israeli supervisor. Although both therapist and supervisor ostensibly work in a psychodynamic way, the supervisor wants immediately to give the patient

1 I have chosen to adopt the authors' phrase "settler-colonial" in this review. Substituting my own phrase, a choice that might be recommended in reviewing another book, would be, here, to replicate the violence that the book seeks to expose.

Richard Grose
rgrose93@gmail.com


medication for anxiety although the therapist wants to hear what the patient has to say. When the patient refuses medication, the treatment continues with Amjad turning sessions into obsessive recitations of his anxieties. As the treatment continues, Amjad begins talking about specific moments in which he has felt suffocated, many of which relate to his experiences with Israeli military and police. At this point, the supervisor indicates that it is time to terminate treatment. When the therapist relays this to the patient, Amjad explodes in anger at the therapist's proposal to abandon their work. Deciding not to terminate a treatment that was deepening, the therapist then works without supervision. Soon after this, Amjad says that the ball in his throat is really his hatred of himself. This leads to his relating a story that occurred two years prior of his driving his then-seven-year-old daughter, who was in an exuberant, happy mood, to a birthday party. At a checkpoint, there is a delay because of protesters throwing stones at the Occupation troops. When Amjad asks a soldier if his daughter can use the bathroom, the soldier, pointing his gun at him, says, "Get back in your car and tell your daughter to piss herself in the car." Hugging his devastated daughter, Amjad drives home and notices for the first time a ball forming in his throat.

I relate this case history because it reflects so much of what this book is about. We see Amjad's and his daughter's attempt to lead normal lives being destroyed in a moment of reflexive Israeli cruelty. We see the Israeli supervisor viewing the Palestinian patient through the filter of her life as an Israeli, which prevents her from being curious about the mind of the patient and prompts her to terminate the treatment as soon as the Occupation comes up in the material. We see a Palestinian therapist, following the principles of psychoanalytic listening to the point where her patient can reveal to her the traumatic moment when his symptom appeared. And we see how in Palestine the Occupation comes into the consulting room.

On the subject of the Occupation, by the end of the book, we have read discussions of "unchilding as a system," or the systematic destruction of "the joy and playfulness of a child [which] stands in opposition to the realities of settler colonialism as a violent structure that assiduously works to make itself present and felt at every moment (p.54)." In other words, in "an apartheid system of institutional psychological violence," the treatment of Amjad's daughter, "to strip her of humanity and dignity, to paralyze her, to humiliate her (p.55)" is indeed the point of the system, together with destroying her father's power to protect her. A system designed to destroy the psyches of the occupied people is termed here a "necropower," where death, physical and psychological, is not "an unfortunate by-product of a political 'conflict' or inevitable consequence of draconian but necessary security measures (p.55)" but rather the very point of the Occupation.

In conditions of the Occupation, this book argues, where the entire force of the state aims to destroy the basic psychological structures of life (represented by this father and daughter), suicide can take on a very different meaning than it does in other circumstances. Suicide in Palestine can be the refusal to participate in the slow death that the state makes of life, and it is often aimed at asserting the very values that the settler-colonial power strives to eliminate, namely, the possibility that individual Palestinians can act on their own behalf, protesting what the authors term the necropower that holds all Palestinians in its grip, and asserting the possibility of a community of values that can exist only in violent protest against the violence of this necropower. Suicide statistics are cited in the book as evidence of social breakdown under the Occupation, but suicide is also seen as potentially expressive and positive in affirming social values that are under systematic attack. "These acts of self-realization are in response to a sustained hegemonic structure of settler-colonial violence engineered to atomize individuals, attempting to strip them of their communities, their identities, and their internal ego coherence. That is, their actions are a reaction to sociopathic settler-colonial structures (p. 92)." Seeing suicide as affirmation within a reality systematically designed to destroy the soul is one challenge this book presents to classical psychoanalysis, which, it is important to remember, was born in comfortable bourgeois circumstances.

The second focus of the book is psychoanalysis under the conditions of the Occupation. The authors make two points, both full of meaning for psychoanalytically informed readers: they show psychoanalysis in Palestine to be placed in the service of both oppression and liberation.

First, oppression. They show that psychoanalytic thinking is used by the Israeli settler-colonial power as ideological support for their aims. One use is psychoanalytic diagnosis to pathologize resistance. A Palestinian who is experiencing anger is seen as regressing to the paranoid-schizoid position; the diagnosis here denies the reality that a Palestinian has every reason to be angry with her life as determined by Israel. One Palestinian clinician, however, put it in broader terms: "If one is compelled to name a psychological symptom, [one is] often avoiding the language of the patient [...] Diagnosing is a blockage (a checkpoint) to accessing the language of the patient. Diagnosis increases alienation (p.66)."

Another such use is "dialogue." The authors make clear that a "dialogue" between the colonizers and the colonized that presumes the parties are equals denies reality and can only normalize the colonial situation. Thus "dialogue," which in the psychoanalytic context is viewed as a positive thing, talking/verbalizing, in the Palestinian context connotes the disavowal of the reality of the Occupation.

A further use of psychoanalytic terms to mask reality is the use of the term "neutrality." The authors quote Martin Kemp that "psychoanalysis, predicated on the assumption of neutrality of the analyst, 'disguises a firm support for the denied, but systemic, racialized violence that characterizes inter-community relations in Palestine/Israel (p. 116, emphasis in the original).'" The authors term this use of psychoanalysis "psychoanalytic innocence." Finally, they show that whenever clinicians or organizations are challenged in their use of psychoanalysis as described here, the response is one of anger (p. 118).[2]

Second, liberation. Psychoanalysis is also wielded in Palestine as an instrument of liberation, for life and against the death drive of the Israeli settler-colonial project. The authors begin with Franz Fanon, who said that "the role of the clinic and the psychiatric hospital must be an institution of disalienation (p. 183)." They discovered in Palestine a network of "autonomous clinics that serve exclusively Palestinian populations (p.183)," in other words, clinics in Palestine that aim precisely at disalienation by withdrawing from institutional ties to the Israeli clinical system.

The authors write, "The social and professional relations between clinics and clinicians not only produce knowledge for the maintenance of livability and sumud.[3] They also produce a network of practice and care that constitute an autonomous national space for Palestinian livability, affirmation, and indeed reality checking (p. 184)." An autonomous national space. The authors are clear about the absence of any politics in the region. Any real politics would have to be based on shared understandings of the nonviolent ways power is distributed. Palestine lives without politics, that is, with violence. But the Palestinian clinical world, under the circumstances of the radical elimination of any real politics, has created a psychoanalytically based space that shows as clearly as perhaps any psychoanalytic entity since "Freud's Free Clinics"[4] the liberatory implications in psychoanalysis.

It should also be said, as it is several times in the book, that although Palestinian clinicians are open to exploring the "realities of the Israeli settler colony" with their Palestinian patients, they do not reduce all complaints to that. Returning to the subject of suicide, they indicate that suicide can be either a "political act of freedom" or "a neoliberal outcome of individualist narcissism and self-interest (p. 200)." In holding both interpretations open—social/political protest and individual psychopathology—they are, I would argue, practicing a form of neutrality, but they seemingly can hardly say so, given the appropriation of that word by psychoanalytic innocence.

Finally, a personal note. Although my support for the Palestinian cause in the current situation was complete and entire when I picked up this book, reading the descriptions of the suffering of Palestinian patients both from social as well as intrapsychic sources and the many compelling stories of Palestinian clinicians who do their best for their patients under extremely difficult circumstances, I was struck by my own reaction. Indeed, I became aware that I had unconsciously introjected some of the Israeli settler-colonial mind-set when I noted my surprise in reading about the inner worlds of Palestinian patients and clinicians. I learned from this book that I, too, had unconsciously adopted a shallow view of Palestinians either as victims or fighters but not as people with inner lives. For this alone I am very grateful to the authors. ■

2 The International Association for Relational Psychoanalysis and Psychotherapy "violently shut down 'debate' within its international membership, who were urging the organization to move its annual conference from Tel Aviv (p. 118)."

3 The authors cite community psychologist and anthropologist Lena Meari on the subject of sumud, an Arabic word denoting the inner attachments that Palestinians can call upon to maintain themselves psychologically both when in Israeli prisons and in the larger prison that are the occupied territories. She sees it a "psychological act of both defiance and willful self-affirmation through healthy attachments to one's internal and social world (p. 148)."

4 Elizabeth Ann Danto, *Freud's Free Clinics: Psychoanalysis and Social Justice*, 1918-1938 (New York: Columbia University Press, 2005).

# IP Books

*Jew-Hating: The Black Milk of Civilization*

Edited by Merle Molofsky

This is a rich, intriguing, and often innovative collection of essays regarding anti-Semitism, opened by Celan's startling poem "Death Fugue." Many of the chapters were written in response to the first paper by Arnold Richards, dealing with "Freud's godlessness," but they also open additional new horizons. The twenty authors—psychoanalysts, psychologists, psychiatrists, and creative artists—bring up social, theological, and political perspectives on their topics. The historical perspective discussed starts from ancient Greek and Roman cultures, touches upon the origins of Christianity, often focuses on Freud and his early circle, and leads to the Holocaust and to contemporary American society. Any reader interested in these issues will find here sophisticated food for thought. —*Emanuel Berman, PhD, University of Haifa and the Israel Psychoanalytic Society*

**For more information or to purchase this book:**

Visit ipbooks.net/product/jew-hating-the-black-milk-of-civilization or scan the QR code

IPBOOKS.NET

# room LIVE GALA 2023

## July 13, 2023

**8pm EDT • Via Zoom**

Honoring

**DEBORAH DANCY**
Multimedia abstract artist

**KARIM DAJANI**
Clinical psychologist & psychoanalyst

**LINDA MICHAELS**
Co-founder, Psychotherapy Action Network (PsiAN)

**JANICE MUHR**
Co-founder, Psychotherapy Action Network (PsiAN)

Thank you to our supporters!*

Aisha Abbasi
Graciela Abelin-Sas Rose, MD
Dana Bilsky Asher
Donna Bassin
Kristen Miller Beesley
Phyllis Beren
Ofra Bloch
Martha Bragin
Joseph Cancelmo
Margaret (Polly) Carter
Eric Chasalow & Barbara Cassidy
Deborah Choate
William Cornell
Sophia Coudenhove
Ellyn Daniels
Kate Daniels
Mary Louise DeNardo
Pascale Denis
Michael Diamond
Fang Duan
Leslie Deutsch
Carolyn Ellman
Laura Farha
Judith Felton
Janet Fisher
Iris E Fodor
Len Follick
Margaret Fulton
Patricia Gianott
Mia Goldman
Adam Goldyne
Francisco J. Gonzalez
Joanna Goodman
Herbert Gross
Gary Grossman
Forrest Hamer
Elizabeth kandall
Maurine Kelly
Paula Kliger
Marilyn Kohn
Michael Krass
Harold Kudler
Lynne Layton
Jane Lazarre
Jeanne Parr Lemkau
Ronnie Lesser
Jaime Levine
Joan Levine
Judith Levy
Susannah Lewis
Maria Longuemare
Ellen Luborsky
Cindy Lucas
Kerry Malawista
Ellen Marakowitz
Mary Margaret McClure
Diane Meier
John Minahan
Julia Moore
Paula Moreci
Lizbeth Moses
Sally Moskowitz
Janice Muhr
Hattie Myers
Ruth Neubauer
Jenifer Nields
Charles Noyes
Rachael Peltz
Ava Bry Penman
Tessa Peteete
Billie A. Pivnick
Christie Platt
Psychotherapy Action Network
Reem Abdul Qadir
Elizabeth Reese
Kathryn Rickard
Beth Rourke
Sandy Ryan
Francesca Schwartz
Ronnie M. Shaw
Alexandra Shinn
Susan Siegeltuch
Betsy Spanbock
Patti Spencer
Aneta Stojnic
Kelsey Stager
Sara Taber
Mary Tirolo
Anne Warren
Sara Weber
Kaja Weeks
Leni Winn
Josephine Wright
Patricia Wright
Jane Yates

We would also like to thank the 30 contributors who prefer to remain anonymous.

*As of July 13, 2023

DONATE: ANALYTIC-ROOM.COM/GALA2023

Printed in the USA
CPSIA information can be obtained
at www.ICGtesting.com
LVRC090720150923
758081LV00003B/5

* 9 7 8 1 9 6 0 6 8 0 0 5 1 *